Hispanic Marketing Grows Up

D1532021

OTHER MARKETING BOOKS FROM PMP

The Kids Market: *Myths & Realities*

Marketing to American Latinos, Part I

Marketing to American Latinos, Part II

The Whole Enchilada

Beyond Bogedas: *Developing a Retail Relationship with Hispanic Customers*

The Mirrored Window: *Focus Groups from a Moderator's Point of View*

The Great Tween Buying Machine

Marketing Insights to Help Your Business Grow

Why People Buy Things They Don't Need

A Knight's Code of Business: *How to Achieve Character and Competence in the Corporate World*

India Business: *Finding Opportunities in this Big Emerging Market*

Moderating to the Max! *A Full-tilt Guide to Creative Focus Groups and Insightful Depth Interviews*

Marketing to Leading-Edge Baby Boomers

Clear Eye for Branding: *Straight Talk on Today's Most Powerful Business Concept*

Advertising to Baby Boomers

What's Black About It?: *Insights to Increase Your Share of a Changing African-American Market*

Marketing to the New Super Consumer: Mom & Kid

Hispanic

EXPLORING PERCEPTIONS

Marketing

AND FACING REALITIES

Grows Up

Asi Viene el Sandwich.
That's the Way the Sandwich Comes.

JUAN FAURA

PMP

PARAMOUNT MARKET PUBLISHING, INC.

Paramount Market Publishing, Inc.
301 S. Geneva Street, Suite 109
Ithaca, NY 14850
www.paramountbooks.com
Telephone: 607-275-8100; 888-787-8100   Facsimile: 607-275-8101

Publisher: James Madden
Editorial Director: Doris Walsh

Cataloging in Publication Data available
ISBN 0-9766973-4-3

Paramount Market Publishing books are available at special quantity discounts to use for sales promotions, employee premiums, or
educational purposes. For more information or to order please call
888-787-8100, e-mail jim@paramountbooks.com or write to PMP,
Inc.,301 S. Geneva Street, Suite 109, Ithaca, NY 14850.

Contents

For Juan Antonio Faura—
my father and the best marketer I will ever know

Acknowledgments

I N MY LAST BOOK, I tried to make sure I covered everyone that contributed to the writing of the book in some way, but as I expected, I missed a couple of pretty important people and I didn't spend as much time as I should have on a couple of others that have played an incredibly important role in getting us to where we are today.

The first person I missed was my beloved sister Belinda. She is my oldest sibling and she has always been incredibly supportive of everything I have done, even when I was a dumb junior high punk with dumb junior high punk ideas. To her I say: I love you and you know I will always remember and appreciate how patient and loving you have been, thank you. I also neglected to mention or acknowledge Christopher Ireland, the CEO of Cheskin while I was there. My departure from Cheskin definitely created some strain between Christopher and I, but an acknowledgement section for a business book written by me that does not mention her and what she has afforded me in the growth of my career would be incomplete and not really honest. Christopher, thank you for helping me to understand that the most effective way to defy convention in business is through brilliance and thank you most of all for showing me that the best way to get people to feel passionately about the company they work for is by empowering them as professionals and caring for them as people.

The people that I did not spend nearly as much time acknowledging as I should have were my wife Sara, Gabriel Garcia, Warren Harmel, Tony Dieste and Greg Knipp. Sara, nothing I could write will ever be enough acknowledgment. Gabriel was the third employee of my company and moved from California to pursue this crazy dream on nothing more than my idea and our friendship. Thank you for your trust, your courage and most of all your incredible work. Tony, thank you for having the confidence in me and my crazy ideas to actually afford me a platform to create something special and thank you for all of the advice and patience over the years. Warren, I want to thank you for all the times over the years that you have lent me your ear when I came up with new concepts and for sharing your experience with me to help me refine those concepts. Last but not least I want to thank Greg Knipp, my partner in Cultura and the only person I could imagine doing this with. Thank you for your cool head and your patience. Cultura would not be what we are today without your balancing influence and diplomacy, none of which are worth nearly as much to me as your friendship. I also want to thank you and Warren Harmel on behalf of all of those that have made the point over the years that to be truly successful in Hispanic marketing in the U.S., being a great marketer counts far more than being Hispanic.

Here's to Frances, to you, and to your new baby!

—J. F.

Introduction

AS I WAS THINKING about what to call the book I came up with myriad considerations that would influence my decision. Of course I wanted the title of the book to be so intriguing that it would incite enough curiosity in people that they might actually buy and read it. It had to reflect the raw quality of some of the things I wrote about, but it also had to have that conversational, everyday tone with which I always try to infuse my writing. As I was thinking about it, someone also brought up the fact that the name should somehow reflect the journey that fueled many of the ideas and thoughts contained within the book. In their effort to help me, some of the folks at the agency suggested that I think about my travels and try to come up with things that stuck in my mind.

As you can imagine, that encompassed a host of different conversations, places, sights, and all kinds of things. The thing that stuck most in my mind and which I actually mention later on in the book is a town in New Mexico by the name of Truth or Consequences. I can't begin to imagine the story that goes along with how that town was named. In any case, it is that town and its name that came popping up time and again when I thought about the trip.

What I am talking about in this book is precisely that the truth about the Hispanic market *and* the consequences that sharing the truth might have for me and others who make our living understanding the market. So, although the name of the town is Truth or Consequences—or T&C as it is commonly known—I thought an appropriate name for the book would be *Truth and Consequences* because there would be plenty of both as a result of it.

All the while, however, in thinking about what to name the book, I also kept coming back to a phrase that I grew up using and still use to this day. It may seem a bit crazy, but follow me here. I really think you'll get it and actually dig it. For those that have seen the movie *Scarface*, I will be taking you back to a very small and really inconsequential part of the movie, but a part I am sure you will remember. For those of you that haven't seen the movie, I will try to frame the situation so you get the picture.

In the movie, Tony Montana, the main character and his best friend Manolo are working at a Cuban café. It is actually just a lunch truck where they serve Cuban food. Anyway, this is their first job in the U.S. and Tony is not happy about having to wash dishes and cut onions and he is complaining to Manolo that his friend, the one who got them the jobs, really screwed them since they got the jobs and their papers by killing someone. During the argument between Tony and Manolo, one of the patrons of the café walks up to Manolo and complains that there is not enough meat in the sandwich and he asks for more meat. Manolo, frustrated and still arguing with Tony looks at the guy and says "*Que mas carne, ni que mas carne, asi viene el sandwich men* (actually pronounced *mein*)." The translation would be: "More meat, what more meat, that's the way the sandwich comes."

Since watching that movie I have always used that phrase whenever I am confronted with situations in which it is life that dictates the outcome. Hurricane Hugo destroyed the house you just saved your whole life to buy? *"Asi viene el sandwich, men."* Your car broke down just when you didn't have any money left from your paycheck *"Asi viene el sandwich, men."* You get the point. The phrase is used when there is no one to complain to, when things are what they are because that is how life has arranged them.

So, in going on the road and having a number of my carefully thought out hypotheses and theories either thoroughly revised or completely wiped out—hypotheses and theories that took years to craft and refine mind you—the only thing I kept thinking was, you guessed it *"Asi viene el sandwich."* Therefore, it seemed almost criminal not to incorporate my beloved turn of phrase into the name of the book and I came up with *Truth and Consequences: That's the Way the Sandwich Comes.* I figured the title would be pretty polarizing so I wanted to provide a bit more fodder for either camp, the love-it camp or the "what-*was*-he-thinking?" camp.

As we were getting closer to printing, my publisher and my sage editor pointed out that while it was entertaining, the title might throw some people for a loop—especially the more buttoned-up, soy milk cappuccino crowd, who might not see the irony in that title. As always their wise counsel, along with estimates of larger sales, served to change my mind. The title we ended up with is a compromise that I think will appeal to all. By the way, *Asi Viene El Sandwich* was a deal breaker so it got to stay. If you don't get it by the end of the book, then the book itself will probably prove to be of very limited use to you.

1

Hispanic Marketing and Occam's Razor

I F NOTHING ELSE I can pretty much guarantee this will be the only book on Hispanic marketing that draws a parallel between marketing to Hispanics and a theoretical physics theorem. Even if you don't know what Occam's Razor is, I think it will take you no time at all to get my drift.

Occam's Razor is actually rather straightforward and simple. It states that in a situation in which there is more than one right answer, it is the simplest answer that will prove to be most correct. It also states that any explanation for a new phenomenon should be based on what is already known.

Although I believe both elements of this are applicable to the U.S. Hispanic market, it is the former rather than the latter element that is most applicable to marketing to U.S. Hispanics. I included this section because if you get nothing else from this book I want you to understand that marketing to the U.S. Hispanic market is not rocket science. As you move forward in your endeavors you will be surprised how many times the most simple and straightforward explanation yields the answer to many of the questions you have.

When it comes to Hispanic marketing we need to remember those things that make us human because it is most likely those things that will drive the most meaningful ideas. Sometimes the culture is precisely what gets in the way. So, when you are looking for a way to connect meaningfully with the U.S. Hispanic consumer and you are getting multiple answers from multiple sources, remember Occam's Razor. I can guarantee you that of all the explanations and answers you get, it will be the most straightforward and common sense explanation or answer will be the most fruitful.

Saying what needs to be said

I was in the middle of writing my second book, a follow up to *The Whole Enchilada*, when this book just pushed itself to the front. I should qualify that and say although the book was most definitely residing somewhere in the depths of my crazy mind, a number of things helped it along. I had an opportunity to get back on the speaking "circuit" and found it to be one of the most satisfying and meaningful times of my career. I was lucky enough to be invited to speak at dozens of venues and in front of very diverse audiences. As you can imagine, any time you speak before an audience it is a somewhat unnerving experience. I don't care how many times you have done it, public speaking always stirs butterflies and if it doesn't, you shouldn't be up there in the first place. The way I see it you should only get up to speak when you have something meaningful to say.

Throughout my career I have always tried to be careful never to make one of these speaking opportunities a glorified sales pitch for my agency. If people like what I have to say and they think there may be a fit, they can easily find Cultura or me. So, every time I speak, I do so with the sincere desire to leave the audience thinking and asking questions they might not have thought of before, or more important, leave them with something they can actually use to help their businesses.

What has made the last few months a bit more meaningful and satisfying is that I am fresh off the road after having spoken with hundreds of the people I purport to know something about. Over the years, I have had the fortune of speaking with thousands of Hispanics from all sorts of backgrounds about a variety of subjects. Those conversations have been the fodder for the ideas and insights I have shared with my clients and readers. They have also been the fuel for my undying insistence that the work that comes out of my agency is truly reflective of what the consumer wants.

Almost all of those earlier conversations were a part of a designed project commissioned by a client for a specific purpose. In those instances there was always a quota, a specified and defined objective. You can imagine that in the course of human interaction there are a lot of things that come to the surface and a lot of thoughts and ideas that are a part of that interaction that go far beyond the specified objective. I always tried to squeeze as much humanity as I could out of these natural interactions.

Nevertheless it was always someone else's dime we were working on, and we had to focus on our objective.

The trip I just undertook, however, was all mine. We had no quotas, no guides, no specific objectives, just my cameraman, the road, and as many Hispanics as we could run into between San Diego and Boston. We talked about everything: politics, sex, money, rock and roll, and whatever else occurred to the people with whom I spoke.

I went on this journey because I feel we have come to a point in Hispanic marketing in the U.S. where the rubber meets the road and the curves are going to get a bit hairy. We have been doing this long enough to know that clients, consumers, and media and marketing professionals involved with Hispanic marketing either know what they are doing or they do not. It sounds obvious, but unfortunately our sense of self-preservation has made it more complicated than that.

The Moment

We are about to go down a path that to my knowledge hasn't been walked when it comes to Hispanic marketing and cultural understanding in the U.S., so I would like to spend just a minute sharing with you, on a more personal level, why I decided to take this road trip. I want to be perfectly clear about why I did this. And to a certain extent, how I did it.

Why the Trip?

Spring–Summer 2004

After about a week of working myself up for it, I finally sat down to write the collection of personality profiles that would make up the follow-up book to *The Whole Enchilada*. I was pretty confident about this one. After all, I had one book under my belt and had gotten very positive feedback on the section that featured the various personality profiles of potential Hispanic customers. So I sat down and was able to write two profiles and was on the way to writing my third when I hit the wall. This was not your run of the mill writer's block either. This came along with an epiphany thrown in as a bonus. I was trying to write the third profile and I came up blank, but not in the usual way a writer might be unable to think of his next plot twist or character flaw. What I was writing after all, while a work of fiction, was supposed to be grounded in actual experience, knowledge, and insight about the people I was writing about. At first I thought it was a case of simple writer's block, but I soon realized that it was something more serious than writer's block; it was a lack of raw material from which to create the profiles.

As you can imagine, when you begin a labor of love like this and come to a serious crossroad, you take a step back and think about it. So that's exactly what I did. I took a step back and worked it through. This is when the epiphany came. I had miscalculated a key aspect of what I was doing. I had made the assumption that because I was a U.S. Hispanic market expert, I would be able to come up with more than enough material to build these characters. I thought that since I had spoken to thousands of Hispanics across a range of markets, age segments, and socioeconomic backgrounds through a host of research projects over the years I would have the raw knowledge to build enough profiles to give the U.S. Hispanic market a human face. I figured that my background in research provided me with enough insights to be able to say that I was an expert without batting an eye. Based on what our industry defines as an expert, the truth is that I do qualify as one.

The problem for me is that it felt dishonest. I did not feel like an expert sitting there thinking, "You know what, I really don't know what the U.S. Hispanic market looks like, what it sounds and smells like, what it feels like."

On the ground in towns across the U.S.—the *whole* United States —Hispanic lives are shaping our culture every day. What those of us who are "experts" base our assertions and insights on is not, to me, the true representation of the U.S. Hispanic market. What we base our knowledge on, knowledge we share with our clients, is founded on designed pieces of research covering specific geographies, age segments, language dominance, categories and so on. Because of that, by definition, the insights we have gained have come through what to me feels like artificial and limited means.

Don't get me wrong. I have yet to come across any high quality, custom-designed research project that did not yield good and useful information. It is just that for what I wanted to do, that type of knowledge and insight wasn't working. What I wanted was to bring the U.S. Hispanic market to life. I wanted to paint a full, human, and bright picture of the U.S. Hispanic market to share with our clients and others who might be interested, but might not know a thing about the Hispanic market. I wanted to be able to call myself a real expert in who and what the U.S. Hispanic market is in human terms, in everyday terms with no need to pitch new business, build campaigns, or convince corporate America to spend more money on reaching Hispanics.

I realized that if I could establish a human image of the Hispanic market and build a compelling business case around it in the mindset of corporate America, the money would follow. As I was going through this little Jerry Maguire–like moment, the second and more powerful part of the epiphany hit me. If I felt this way after talking with thousands of Hispanics over many years, what was happening with those who were also calling themselves experts, but may not have had the benefit of all those conversations?

I came to the scary conclusion that the image of our culture being promulgated across our industry was based solely on personal experience (I am; therefore I know.), having attended a few focus groups (How different can Hispanics from other countries in other places be?) or God forbid (Trust us, this is really what they all watch and listen to.).

This last part and my aversion to feeling like I was misrepresenting myself is what spurred me to do something about it. But what? What can you do other than design and execute research addressing the U.S. Hispanic market and use the reports those studies yield to build your insights and hypotheses? This was a difficult question to answer, but as with most difficult questions, the answer was simple. Go out and talk to Hispanics. Just go and talk to them.

The next question was how to do it. I had already determined that it would definitely not be a traditional research project in which you recruit the people you will be talking to. I wanted to go on the road across the U.S. talking to many Hispanics and filming them when possible. So I pulled out a map and decided I would go from corner to corner, starting in San Diego right at the U.S.–Tijuana border crossing and going to Massachusetts. Being the president of an ad agency, however, posed some serious challenges that I would have to tackle along the way. While I would have loved to go out and do this all in one shot, going straight through from San Diego to Boston would prove to be impossible. My compromise was to extend planned business trips and meetings to cover the region I happened to be in. If I happened to have a meeting in New York for example, I would stay in New York for a week and then drive through New Jersey, Connecticut, New Hampshire, Rhode Island and finally Massachusetts. It was not how I would like to complete the project, but it would have to do in order to keep the agency and marital harmony going. So now that you know the deep-down why and a bit of the how, let's get rolling.

2

Trust Me, I'm Hispanic

I T USED TO BE that we felt good about ourselves because we were the emissaries of great news to companies desperately looking for fertile ground. Way back when, before the "The-census-numbers-said-what?" moment, we were in a comfortable and lucrative niche without having to do much evolving. All of a sudden, we were Hispanic marketing professionals—experts in the fastest growing, second largest, $600 billion dollar-buying-power population in the United States.

Looking back, I think I can trace the Hispanic awakening to a single moment in the vast landscape of American consciousness. I would love to say that this awakening was sparked in a single moment by a speech like the one given by Barack Obama at the Democratic National Convention, perhaps given by the now-senator son or daughter of Hispanic immigrants who made it here by the skin of their teeth. No such thing took place, however. What did take place was the lackluster 1999 Grammy Awards taken over completely by Ricky Martin. The number of articles, talk-show invitations, and calls to my office that performance generated has been unequaled to this day. I was watching the show and I can tell you it still brings a smile to my face to remember it. As I said, the show had been nothing to write mom about when Ricky came on to perform "The Cup of Life," the song written for the 1998 World Cup.

As I watched people get on their feet to dance I was thinking to myself, "This is going to change everything," and indeed it did. That performance was followed by the 2000 Census numbers, which as we all now know, blew every estimate for Hispanic population growth out of the water. After that our world changed because, like it or not, we had the country's attention focused squarely on us. Marketing vice-presidents everywhere were asking, "What are we doing about this Hispanic thing?" and we were all there to answer the call. We shared our collective "Hispanicness" in reports, conferences, research, and a variety of other ways, not unlike what we are doing today.

There is an incredible difference between then and now. It has taken longer than I thought it would, but it has finally come to pass. In our desire to help our clients tap into the huge opportunity the U.S. Hispanic market represented, we neglected to establish a litmus test—a standard below which we would not agree to work. The difference between then and now is simple: results. It used to be that when you hadn't been doing anything to target the second largest population in the U.S., doing anything was better than doing nothing at all. Those were the days when companies were satisfied to be doing something, anything.

Then we evolved and realized that wasn't necessarily true. If all you were willing and able to do was just put a Spanish sound track to U.S. talent, you might be better off doing nothing at all. The sophistication of the advertising we developed evolved right along with the sophistication of the consumers. We came up with award-winning advertising and watched as the number of media vehicles on which to play those commercials multiplied.

This brings us to where we are today. We are a part of a thriving industry that has grown from about 40 established U.S. Hispanic advertising and marketing agencies in 1996 to well over 200 in 2005. We have witnessed the evolution of a culture. Yet in the middle of the first decade of the 21st century we have made little progress in evolving our industry to match the evolution of the culture.

Our clients are now actually demanding results; can you imagine the gall? It has taken almost ten years to go from anything is better than nothing to expecting your investment to pay off. That is way too long for me, particularly since we are still not moving forward the way we should be. It is this lack of progress that has frustrated me and it is this lack of progress I am seeking to address. I fully realize that a lot of what is written in this book will rub people the wrong way, but as I said, *asi viene el sandwich.*

Portraits

Ernesto (Ernie) Gomes
Age 45, Albuquerque, New Mexico

My name is Ernesto Gomes. Yes that's Gomes, pronounced "Goams." It's not Gomez. I know the name probably originated as Gomez, but somewhere down the line one of my ancestors changed it to Gomes and that is what we have kept it.

I am an engineer in a local construction firm and I have three children. I am also aware that we are of Hispanic origin, although our family comes originally from Spain. We are not Mexican like most people think we are. I do not speak Spanish, nor do I have the desire to. I have not had any of my children learn Spanish, although two of them have learned it on their own. My parents did not speak Spanish and they taught me and my brothers that we live in the U.S. and we should therefore speak English. I have asked my children to speak in English when they are in the house.

I know it must seem like I am ashamed of being Hispanic, but that's not the case at all, it's just that all Hispanics are not cut from the same cloth. In this country people think that we are all waiters or gardeners or maids and we are not. We also did not all come from Mexico, although people think we did. Every single week I see something that upsets me about Hispanics in the U.S., especially now that there is so much attention being paid to the Hispanic population.

What is the big deal, they make it seem like we just got here or something when in reality we have been here for a long time

---

Portraits presented here are composites of people I interviewed on my trip. None is intended to represent a particular person.

and the Hispanic or actually the Spanish influence is written all over this country. You doubt it? Why don't you take a quick look at a map and read all those names for all those states like Nevada, Arizona, Oregon, Montana, Indiana and I could go on. Now I sound like I am really proud of being Hispanic, but that's not the case either. Actually, I don't refer to myself as Hispanic, I don't think of myself as Hispanic and I tell my children that they should not limit themselves to thinking of themselves as Hispanics.

You should also know that here in New Mexico Hispanics are divided into very distinct and different groups. One group falls into what my family and I fall into, more European or Spanish than anything else and then there is the other part of the population, the population that does come over the wall. I will tell you that one of the things that pissed me off the most for a long time when I started working for the firm that I work for is that someone would always come to me and say "Hey Ernie can you tell these guys to do this or to do that." What the hell were they thinking? I don't even speak Spanish. I told them that too. People know better now. I know that there are other Hispanics in the company that resent my position, but to be honest I don't really care. When I see what I see in the Hispanic population here in New Mexico I'm glad I have this point of view.

I know I probably don't need to say this, but obviously I do not watch or listen to any Spanish language television or radio. I also don't particularly care for getting marketing materials in Spanish; it upsets me. Just because someone thinks my name looks or sounds kind of Hispanic they assume I want to receive something in Spanish and it couldn't be further from the truth. The way I see it, market to me like you would market to anyone else if you really want my business. Don't try to "connect" with me through my culture because brother, I can tell you, you know nothing about my true culture or what it is all about.

Some people also get upset at me because of my views about illegal immigration, but like most everything else, I don't really care what other people think, particularly the militant Hispanics that get the most upset. What is so hard about understanding that when people come into the country without papers they are breaking the law? It's as simple as that. I don't care what they are coming here to do; they are coming in illegally to do it and they are consuming resources that me and my family are paying for. The fact that Hispanics sit there and claim that all these people want is to come in and work hard to provide for their families is beside the point; that's not what makes it illegal. I am a strong supporter of the Republican Party and I will support anything that helps to fight illegal immigration.

3

Why Can't We Make Progress?

The Right Spend, the Wrong Idea

We get together at conferences and talk about how corporate America has not yet caught up with the true potential of the U.S. Hispanic market and we wonder why. We commiserate with each other about how so many of our clients have recent MBA graduates with no real experience working on their Hispanic business and how we don't have access to the top and we wonder why. We think the reason top management does not pay enough attention to us is because they are not putting enough money into the effort. As long as the Hispanic initiative is a rounding error no one at the "O" level (CEO, CFO, CMO, CIO, and so forth) will pay attention. So, to answer this particular "why?", we come up with what we think will be the tipping point in our favor. We come up with an industry-sponsored report about what the right spend should be. This report basically establishes a minimum baseline of spending per category to target the U.S. Hispanic market. Once the spending for the category overall is established, the report then applies several factors including Hispanic household spending for the category. We then come through the door of our clients' offices, report in hand with a big smile on our faces, righteously saying, "See, I told you the problem was we just weren't spending enough." And we wonder why we can't get anywhere.

The problem is that for the most part our clients know what they are doing and they know that we cannot possibly be certain about the right spend based solely on a report that has nothing to do with their brand, their specific market situation, their market cycle, and their target definition. A report, by the way, that will directly benefit the sponsors of it financially for some time to come. How on earth can we possibly talk so broadly about the right spend with any credibility?

As marketing professionals we *should* know that the right spend is the level at which our clients achieve maximum return on investment based on their bottom lines, period. We *should* know that regardless of ethnicity or language preference, we need to analyze the fit between brand and consumer. We *should* know that we will probably need to do a market test to determine that optimum level of spending and only after we obtain results from that test can we talk about the right spend. Actually, even after you run an in-market test you need to determine the demographic and psychographic match of your target with the national rollout markets to see if the test is really applicable on a national level.

We should and actually do know these things as marketing professionals. The problem is that some time ago we stopped being just marketing professionals and became *Hispanic* marketing professionals. At some point we began to let our Hispanicness get in the way of those things we know as marketers. As you can see, I keep saying WE. The reason for that is that I absolutely include myself in that group of Hispanic marketing professionals that looks for the raw data to:

> Some time ago we stopped being just marketing professionals and became Hispanic marketing professionals.

a. Persuade my client to spend more money.

b. Give a reason for why the campaign did not work.

c. Or, entice companies to begin spending on the Hispanic market in the first place.

I don't think we do it with anything other than the best intentions to help our clients, but unfortunately for us using this type of information to further our point actually sets us back and erodes our credibility as marketing professionals. I am writing this because frankly I get tired of standing in front of clients with the latest report's results saying, "Except in your case because our target is different." Or, "Except in your case because our distribution network is different." Or, "Except in your case _____ ," (fill in the blank).

This all came together because we have a client with a very narrow "sweet spot" target definition. This client is all about fresh ideas. It has established itself in the U.S. market in five short years and wants to reach out to the growing Hispanic market. This client sees the opportunity clearly because no company, specifically none of its competitors, have done anything of substance in the market. The space in which it functions is still theirs to win when it comes to the Hispanic market. So we dutifully put together a proposal to go into one test market across a range of media. We planned to cut across all media so that afterwards we could determine what the most efficient media mix and weight should be for its national plan.

As most of us do, we left the budget pages to the latter part of the presentation. Along with our proposal came figures for what they should spend in this market in order to get some lift. It just so happens that this client's product has a long acquisition cycle. The consumer is not going to go out and buy its product the next day. For them immediate lift is measured mostly through brand awareness and affinity. Those were the measures the client gave us to work with. We got to the budget page and one of the clients, a media consultant, said, "How do you know that's the right amount to spend?" It was a valid and important question given our little scenario.

Our media director, being the absolute and consummate professional he is, had gotten competitive spending data as well as numerous other figures provided by the various media we wanted to use. He stood up and provided our clients with all of that information. After he was finished I looked to the client that had asked the question and I knew what he was going to say even before he opened his mouth. "I understand all of that, but how do you know that's the right amount to spend?"

At this point I interrupted and told our client that although all of these figures provided us with some guidelines we did not really know if this was the right spend. I explained we were trying to establish a baseline from which we could then develop plans. I also explained that since no one had actually spent much in the category at all, we had no real competitive comparison. This was important because while it communicated a challenge to us, it also clearly conveyed the opportunity for them. After this explanation the client smiled, said, "Fair enough." and we moved on. He didn't want me to assure him that this was in fact the right amount to spend in the market. He was smart enough to know that there is no way we could know that. He just wanted to hear us say we did not know that. After this incident, the issue really hit me full on and it has continually irked me enough to do something about it.

I want to clarify something before we go any further because I can already see that this could be misconstrued. Any report by itself is not bad, just like any gun by itself is not bad. They both will just sit there until we pick them up and do something with them. Having information on category spending is always good—always. Having information on household spending is also always good. Claiming that these data or any combination thereof is the *right* anything is not good—not ever. We need to understand that every time we use syndicated data or any report backed or financed by media or by any industry group as the objective *piéce de resistance* on which we can hang our hat, we are risking serious erosion to our credibility.

It's true that we may be lucky and get somebody green around the ears that eats up the information and holds it up to his senior management as proof that they need to be doing something more or something different. But we may also get someone like our friend in the presentation—a seasoned marketing professional that can smell bullshit a mile away and is more than willing to call you and your agency on the carpet over it. If I had stood there and tried to convince the guy that the amount of money we were recommending was the right amount of money for x, y, z reasons I am absolutely sure we would have lost all credibility with him. Everything else we put in front of him would have been tinged with a veneer of BS resulting from that first meeting.

My long-winded point is only to say that we should use data carefully and position it to the client as a directional tool that can help guide some decisions. Make sure you contextualize everything you put in front of the client so that both of you will know where to set your expectations. We need to go back to basics as they say and remember those things that made us good marketers rather than trying to leverage those things that we feel make us good *Hispanic* marketing professionals.

I also have to take the opportunity to tell you that it is incredibly frustrating to me to continually hear "expert" after "expert" on their soapboxes armed with nothing more than a Hispanic last name and an accent. Amazing as it may seem, many of these experts actually cannot speak Spanish all that well. I always wonder. You speak English with a thick Spanish accent and you speak Spanish improperly and with a thick English accent, so what do you speak well, whether it is with or without an accent? Or is it all put on just to sound more legitimate? Well, if the latter is the case let me tell you, you sound really lame and you should stop doing it.

"It's the right thing to do."

I have grown to have a negative physical reaction when I hear these words and I can't tell you how often I hear them in the context of why it is key to develop a multicultural, and specifically, a Hispanic-marketing initiative. We always share the numbers—*always*. We make sure we have every relevant demographic statistic we can get our hands on so we can make our case as to why our clients need us. However, when pushed to the wall, when we are really tested about why our clients need to market to Hispanics in the U.S. the best we can come up with is, "Because it's the right thing to do?" Those may not be the words spoken, but the idea definitely is. And we, once again, wonder why we can't get anywhere.

What we have, on many occasions, shared with our clients, given the numbers, the growth, spending power, percentage of the population, and so forth. It's the right thing to do. And let's face it, for a long time, actually to this day, it works most of the time. Most clients see the numbers, hear the growth figures, smell the political and social air, and wholeheartedly agree: "Yup it's the right thing to do."

Until recently most clients might have said that, but now savvier clients—clients that don't view this through any social or political lens, but rather through a purely business lens—are asking a much tougher, "Why should we do this?" It's a question that will not be answered with anything other than a business case. The growth of the population, the increasing buying power and the potential benefit to most of the companies interested in marketing to Hispanics absolutely should warrant social and political considerations when determining *how* a company should engage, but they most definitely should not be the engine pulling the train of *why* a company should engage.

This realization, like almost everything else in this book came about as a result of learning what many of our clients are thinking and facing within their organizations when it comes to Hispanic marketing. As I said previously, we like to commiserate as to why we cannot get further when it comes to many of our clients and this is a big reason why. Within many organizations' marketing departments, questions are being asked and the right answers are not being given.

> *Within many organizations' marketing departments, questions are being asked and the right answers are not being given.*

For example, a client may comment: "Women, Hispanic or otherwise, are a distinct group of consumers that significantly outnumbers Hispanics, English, Spanish or bilingual. They are also a minority recognized by the federal government and we are not targeting them as a distinct segment, so why should we be targeting Hispanics at all if we are not targeting women?" The tempting answer, as you can imagine, is usually a permutation of "Because it's the right thing to do."

The problem is that this is a legitimate business question that has a very sound business reason for being asked, but it does not have the social correctness element embedded in it. However, the fact that we do not provide solid business answers to questions like these does not go unnoticed. Trust me that it is one of the principal reasons that it is hard for us to get an audience with executives higher than a certain level of management. Given the social and political pressures our clients have to deal with, it is not something most of them would be willing to go on record with, but I have had the opportunity to go off record with many of our senior executives and I have come to the conclusion that it is most definitely a significant factor for why we have the issues we do in that regard.

The principal point I want to make with this is that we are advertising, marketing research, and media agencies, not lobbying groups. We do this to help our clients sell their wares, not uphold a social cause, and the more we talk about what we do and what we are recommending our clients to do in a socio-political context, the more walls we will hit. It is not lost on me that what we do and what we want our clients to do has now and will always have a social and political value. How can it not? How can investing in the future of Hispanic children, more access to home loans, investment in social infrastructure, all things that often form a part of the marketing programs we bring to our clients not have social or political value? Of course they do, but they are *not* the reason we are in business. I truly believe that if we focus the way we frame the rationale for everything we do in a business and return-on-investment context we will break down many of the barriers that now limit our access to senior executives, people who can make a difference and ensure the ongoing success of our programs.

> *The more we talk about what we do in a socio-political context, the more walls we will hit.*

One of the other things that has kept us from making significant evolutionary advances when it comes to Hispanic marketing has to do with a very human instinct, self-preservation. In my experience the Hispanic marketing and advertising space has spawned some of the most unique, imaginative, and brilliant thinking within the overall marketing and advertising realm. Although this holds true for every facet of what we do, it is most obvious in the creative space. Some of the most creative advertising anywhere has come from Hispanic minds, both here and in Latin America. I think part of that reason has as much to do with the cynicism that we Latin Americans exercise every once in a while as it does with the very human aspect of dealing with political and social uncertainty for generations. These two things and a healthy sense of humor truly seem to be the recipe for advertising creative that touches us at a very visceral level.

What I wondered though, is why is it that we only get to see flashes of that here in the U.S. and yet we see a constant stream of it coming from Latin America? Why is it that only every once in a while do we see something that leaves us thinking, and more importantly, thinking about the brand it is talking about?

We come back to the whole self-preservation thing. All of us that make our living doing this work are able to do it because we have clients that support us financially. They pay the bills. If it weren't for them, we wouldn't be in business at all, let alone be brilliant. So when our Hispanic creatives come up with something really unique or edgy or completely out there, we as agency owners or managers or directors think to ourselves, "This is incredible, but will it pass my client's jalapeño test? Will it be Hispanic enough?"

Most of our clients at some point have had some sort of exposure to the Hispanic marketing phenomenon and have formed expectations of what Hispanic marketing and advertising creative work should look like. What this expectation is based on depends as much on barometric pressure or the day of the week as it does on any rational or intelligent premise. To be fair, a lot of them do rely on what their Hispanic "experts" tell them the creative should look like. And you want to know the saddest part? Sometimes those "experts" reside in the very agencies where brilliant work is being killed because of them. As senior managers we are interested in "great work" (we say it on our web site right?) but we are even more interested in keeping our agencies open. We know that there is a cost to maintaining integrity and doing what you know to be right and most of the time we are hesitant to incur that cost so we cajole our creatives into "dumbing down" their work, not always mind you, but enough that we notice the difference between what comes from Latin America and what gets done here.

How do we fix this? How can we raise the bar and still keep our clients happy enough to keep our agencies open? Well we begin by realizing that sometimes it is indeed worth losing the business for the sake of having your team believe in what they do and the companies they do it for. Sometimes it is worth it to walk away from money to show that brilliance does indeed have a place in what we do and that there is no price you can put on it. That is what we—the managers, the owners, and the directors—can do, but we are not the only ones that will need to fix this. Brand managers, CMOs, VPs and other marketing executives charged with Hispanic marketing also need to decide if they just want Hispanic work or if they want brilliant work. If they want brilliant work, then they need to get out of the way and stop playing the culture card on the agency they work with.

Sometimes it is worth it to walk away from money to show that brilliance does indeed have a place in what we do and that there is no price you can put on it. If you are a creative and are constantly frustrated by the dilution of your brilliant work, do something about it.

Let the agency decide how much, if any, culture you need for your advertising or marketing to be successful. That's what an agency does or at least that's what it is supposed to do. What do you care if it is Hispanic enough or not? Don't you really care about whether it is actually going to sell your product? Isn't that what should concern both you and your agency? What we do is not about social conscience you know; it is about business. It is about communicating effectively with a potential customer, no more and no less. You will find that if you do indeed get out of the way and let the agency spread its wings, the results will flow naturally. The added advantage of getting out of the way is that you will also quickly see whether your agency has any wings to spread.

If you are a creative and are constantly frustrated by the dilution of your brilliant work, do something about it. Whining that "Account service just doesn't get it . . ." or "Account service are a bunch of pushovers . . ." or my favorite, "The brief is not clear enough . . ." doesn't cut it. Once the owner of the agency or the account director or the strategic planner is willing to go to bat for you, is actually willing to lose an account for you, then what? What will the excuse be then?

When it comes to Hispanic creative talent in the United States and the work they deliver, I think the biggest issue has nothing to do with the actual creative ideation process or the idea development. I have seen some of the most brilliant work across a host of agencies, so it isn't the thinking that is flawed; it's the process and the way the thinking gets delivered that is the problem.

To help in the effort to end mediocrity U.S. Hispanic creatives should try stepping into the shoes of the account director every once in a while. Try for one minute thinking about what it feels like to sit there and have to listen to how the work is just not on strategy when you know that the work is really great and will sell the product. Try listening to the owner of the agency talk about quality out of one side of his or her mouth and keeping the client happy at all costs out of the other. It isn't easy is it? Most of the truly successful breakthrough thinking has come as a result of a symbiotic and mutually organic relationship between account service and creative. In fact, the most successful examples I can think of have been those where throughout the process there were no limitations as to how one or the other should contribute. So in the end let me summarize what I think will be needed to raise our game to the next level.

- *Agency owners, directors, and senior executives:* At some point you will need to show some spine. You will need to show that the quality of the work and the thinking that went into it is more important than money. I am not saying you need to close the agency overnight over a piece of creative, but at some point your people need to see that when you talk about creative and strategic integrity you are sincere. Without that, all the affirmations in the world will not get your folks to believe in you or your company.

- *Marketing executives everywhere:* Check your expectations and assumptions of what and who the Hispanic consumer is. Also check your notions of what will be effective marketing to them. Don't get me wrong. I also know that Hispanic corporate executives are some of the most effective and passionate advocates for Hispanic marketing that works and that breaks with convention, but you can see how someone of the "I-know-because-I-am" camp with his or her own agenda and no clue, can do quite a bit of damage that at some point will have to be undone.

- *Creatives:* Be more open to input from your planner and even, dare I say it, from account service. You don't have to use it, but you should definitely listen. As you move forward in your endeavors try, as much as you can, to frame up and judge absolutely everything you do through the "Will-this-sell-the-product, service-or-brand," lens rather than the "will-it-win-an-award" lens. I know it's hard, especially in instances when the spot that seems to be most effective at doing that seems to be the least creative or edgy spot. Remember that coming up with spots that add to the bottom line is the quickest and most effective way to gain true credibility. Spots that benefit the bottom line will give you more room to come up with the type of creative you want to produce. One of the best ways to do this, in my experience, is to always be able to clearly and easily articulate how it delivers on the strategy. And no, you can't come up with the spot first and then try to retrofit it into the strategy. Time and again, that has proven to be a complete waste of effort. It may not be in the sense that ultimately the ad gets produced, but in the sense that should be the test for everything—did it succeed in making an impact?

Portraits

Luis DiBarelli
Age 38, San Francisco, California

I am Luis DiBarelli and I am from Argentina, originally. I have been in the United States for six years. I was transferred here by the advertising agency I work for. My role in the agency is as a creative. I am now up to being an associate creative director. I do not work for an agency that does advertising for the Hispanic market. Are you crazy? That would be a waste of my talent.

In case you did not know this, some of the best advertising in the world comes from Argentina. Notice I did not say some of the best Hispanic advertising comes from Argentina, I said some of the best advertising period comes from Argentina. Now you know why I think working for a Hispanic advertising agency would be a waste of my talent. The audience for my work would be very limited and I just have worked too hard and have way too much talent for that.

You might have noticed that my last name is DiBarelli, which is clearly not a Hispanic last name. It is actually Italian, which is where my father's family is from. My mother's family is from Germany. Don't ask me how they got to Argentina. I have my ideas, but I don't want to talk about it. Suffice it to say I think it was back in the late 1940s that my father's and mother's families arrived in Argentina. The other thing that might surprise you is the way that I look. I am about 6 feet 1 inch tall and I have blonde hair and blue eyes. You can imagine that every time

---

Portraits presented here are composites of people I interviewed on my trip. None is intended to represent a particular person.

someone finds out I am Hispanic I have to listen to the obligatory, "Gee, you don't look Hispanic." which is very frustrating because in Argentina many people look like I do. I certainly don't stick out because of my looks. It's probably not a big surprise given my European heritage. Now, do not get me wrong at all, because although I have European blood I am completely Argentine and very proud about it. I will tell anybody who asks that I am Argentine. I am also intensely proud of my Spanish. I love being bilingual and I am also very proud of the fact that we actually speak more Castilian Spanish in Argentina.

I watch soccer in Spanish. I don't care where it's from, as long as it is good soccer, which pretty much rules out the MLS. It used to be that I had to settle for watching Mexican soccer 90 percent of the time. Not that it's bad because actually they play excellent soccer in Mexico, but still you know, I wanted to watch some Argentine or Italian or German soccer at times. Now I subscribe to a satellite service that gives me all of those options for an additional cost. I absolutely love it and watch it all the time. I also like watching what everybody else watches in English, *Survivor, American Idol, CSI*, that kind of thing. Other than the soccer I do not have a constant show I like to watch. Well that's not really true; *24* is my favorite show and I like to watch it every time I get a chance. My satellite service also has Discovery and History en Español which I also like to watch when I get the chance. They come with the soccer package.

I'll tell you what I don't watch. I don't watch the programs on the main Hispanic networks like *Don Francisco* or the *novelas*. It's sad that you have to pay extra to get some decent programs, but that's a fact. Because I do watch all the Spanish programming, I do see a lot of Hispanic advertising in the U.S. Some of it is very good, but a lot of it is really awful; I mean really awful. I have to admit that when I see good advertising on Spanish language television I feel good; it makes me proud to see that kind of work running on Spanish-language television here in the United States, which also means my standards have been lowered since coming here. In Argentina I expected to see that kind of advertising all the time.

I also get happy when I see good advertising in English. I guess it's all just a by product of what I do really. Well, maybe not, because there is a little element of added pride when I see it done in Spanish so I guess for me my culture does influence how I feel and how I react to things. Does it make a difference in what I buy? I don't know, maybe. I can't really remember a time when I saw something and immediately had to go out and get whatever they were advertising and I also can't recall a time when I was buying something and I remembered an ad. As creatives, we like to think that's what happens, but we know better. I would say consistent communication is what does the trick; you know having something repeated until it gets ingrained and you remember it almost instinctually.

Other things you might not know about Argentina, but which are very true is that some of the best wine comes from there. There is a particular type of wine, Malbec, which is made from grapes that only grow at certain altitudes and which is absolutely fabulous. We also have the best meat in the world bar none. I don't care where you go you will not find better meat than in Argentina, oh and the beef is not half-bad either (I couldn't resist that one). All kidding aside, we have some of the most beautiful women in the world if I do say so myself.

We also have a little known but often exploited skill, which we utilize whenever it suits us. Argentines can talk loud and I mean really loud in a big group of people and all at the same time. If you have ever heard a group of Argentine men talking about soccer or a bunch of Argentine women talking about politics you know what I am talking about. I think there is a natural aversion to speaking one at a time and frankly it's just boring. What may amaze you is that everyone in the conversation knows what everyone else said and what the issue of discussion was.

When it comes to knowing the answer to everything asked or unasked, Argentines are the only ones that can challenge Cubans. If you ever go out on the town with an Argentine and a Cuban, prepare to take a back seat and just sit back and listen because you are going to be hard pressed to get a word in edgewise.

Am I going to stay in the United States? I don't know. That is the hardest question I am dealing with right now. I make good money, very good money and I could buy a house back in Bariloche the town I am from, but I don't know. Somehow I feel like if I leave I will spend the rest of my life trying to get back to where I am now. Maybe it will depend on whether I meet a beautiful *gringa* and get married and have kids. That would pretty much seal the whole deal for me.

Sometimes I know I come across as pompous and elitist, I know I do, but I can't help it. It is part of being Argentine, what can I tell you. Aside from that I am really funny and will hang out with whomever wants to have a good time.

4

The Language Issue

LL OF US WHO do any work in the Hispanic marketing and media realm have come across the question of how effective it is to market to Hispanics in-language. Clearly advertising in Spanish is called for when you have a consumer that prefers to receive information in Spanish. The effectiveness is obvious in that you are using the consumers' dominant language. The issue, as I have come to realize, is not whether the advertising should be created in Spanish. Rather, it is whether the media that the advertising runs on should also be in Spanish.

It also sounds obvious, doesn't it? I mean if consumers prefer to receive the information in Spanish it stands to reason that where the advertising is placed should, by default, also be in Spanish. This is an assumption that both clients and advertising agencies have made over the years, but talking to people on my trip I found out that it is a wrong assumption.

Here is where I know I am going to get in trouble with my Hispanic, Spanish-language media friends, but as they say, don't shoot the messenger. This is what I heard from people.

The way this came about was as a natural progression of the various conversations I had on the road. Although I did not have a guide or specific objectives I needed to cover, I did have basic questions I wanted to ask of all people, just so I would know in what context to place the conversation. As you can probably anticipate, the basic questions I asked had to do with language preference and media consumption. You know the ones: "What language do you feel most comfortable in?" or "What language do you function in most?" The actual words I used to ask these questions varied, but the gist of the questions was always what you just read.

As a follow up to this question I always asked what language media was watched or listened to most often. I was really asking this question to warm them up, to give them some easy things they could answer and get comfortable with. The answers I got were the very reason I am writing this section.

Like many of my colleagues and clients, I had assumed that the answer to the first question would basically determine the answer to the second question. During this trip I discovered that the assumption has been wrong for all these years. While it is absolutely undisputable that the level of Spanish language media consumption correlates with the language of preference, it is a big mistake to assume that there is an absolute correlation. Let me explain.

Most of the Spanish-dominant or Spanish-preferred people I spoke with told me that yes they do, in fact, consume more Spanish television than English television. So far, so good. As we got deeper into the conversation, however, I began to understand that the margin of preference between Spanish language television and English language television was razor thin. In other words, they preferred to watch Spanish television, but not by much. When it came to Spanish-dominant or Spanish-preferred individuals this margin of difference was relative to the geographic region where we happened to be.

While obviously not scientific in nature, what I found was that in more established U.S. Hispanic markets such as Los Angeles, Miami, New York and Chicago the margin of preference between Spanish language television and English language television was wider than in some of the less developed or established Hispanic markets. And once we understand the reason for the narrow preference it makes all the sense in the world.

All this time we have been under the quite logical assumption that media consumption was based on language fluency and dominance. Spanish-dominant or Spanish-preferred U.S. Hispanics watched or listened to Spanish-language media because that is all they could listen to or watch and understand. Once again we considered it as a black and white issue rather than the various shades of gray that it really is. The reality, like it or not, is that there are not enough descriptors to define how many shades of grey the language dominance issue really falls into. I have always found that the best way to illustrate something like this is with visual aids, models if you will that can represent succinctly what I am talking about. This is no different. I have come up with a visual that should illustrate precisely what I am talking about.

As you will see in the illustration below, the journey between Spanish-only (black) and English-only (white) is a spectrum, a gradient of shades between the two. Below you will also see how we tend to see Hispanics in the U.S. For those of us in the marketing arena, Hispanics in the U.S. are Spanish-dominant, English-dominant, or bilingual. We tend to live in those three defining boxes because frankly, it is the easiest way of addressing the language issue. You can see by comparing the two visual models, that what we have been doing is truly a vast oversimplification of how language actually breaks down.

Spanish	bilingual	English

Most of us function somewhere in the box outlined below. For practical purposes a Hispanic residing more on the left hand side of the gradient can and should be considered Spanish-dominant or Spanish-leaning, while Hispanics residing towards the right side of the gradient can and should be considered English-dominant.

Spanish	English

Source: Cultura

In fairness to all of us, the speed with which market dynamics have changed is remarkable to say the least. All of us in charge of developing relevant communications to address this fast-changing landscape had to come up with an easy-to-handle breakdown of language fluency and we did. But now we need to catch up to where the market is, because the better we understand the ebb and flow of language fluency the better we will be in coming up with a message that has more impact and more media vehicles to show off our great work.

For the purposes of talking to our clients about what segment of the U.S. Hispanic market they needed to target we used the defining framework we came up with, which you see illustrated above. So as we discussed the issue with clients we always talked in terms of the Hispanic consumer being a) Spanish-speaking, b) English-speaking, or c) bilingual. The reality was that we really only talked in terms of either Spanish-speaking or English-speaking, one or the other. Bilingual was a realm that we obviously knew was there, but we also knew that when it came to the U.S. Hispanic market our clients would never consider addressing a bilingual consumer in Spanish or in-culture.

Although I have been writing in the past tense until now, the fact of the matter is that we still talk about the market in these terms—Spanish, English, or bilingual. Bilingual is defined as individuals that can function fluidly in both English and Spanish. Today's reality is that less than 10 percent of the U.S. Hispanic population resides in only one of the boxes.

This means that most Hispanics in the U.S. function somewhere between Spanish-only and English-only. Therefore, the vast majority of the U.S. Hispanic market functions within some form of bilingualism. Now you see where the difficulty comes. Just when you thought you had the language thing down, here comes this guy and screws it all up. Sorry. As I said before, don't kill the messenger. What I have just illustrated for you is what I have heard many times when talking to U.S. Hispanics on the road.

I'll share with you the conversation that finally made me take a closer look at this. As I mentioned before, language fluency, preference, and media consumption were all questions I covered with everybody I talked to. One particular conversation I had was with an articulate and lively woman from Mexico. She explained that she generally spoke Spanish all day long because that is pretty much what her friends spoke. She also mentioned that she had been in the U.S. for over 20 years and had just never gotten the hang of English. This interview was conducted completely in Spanish. So after we established the language usage and preference for her we got into the language she preferred for media, and here is where it started to get interesting. I was completely taken aback when she explained to me that she actually watched more English-language television than Spanish television.

As it is patently clear from her earlier responses, this didn't jibe with her language of preference or dominance so I had to ask her about it. What she explained, and what I subsequently heard over and over again, was that she did indeed watch one *novela* (Mexican soap opera) and the news every night, but that was it when it came to Spanish language television. She also explained that her husband watched all of the highlight shows from the Mexican soccer league. She told me about various shows she had seen and did not care for at all. She didn't like the variety shows that were generally humorous in nature and often featured scantily clad women at some point.

As we progressed in the conversation, I asked her what she actually did watch. Mind you all of the questions and answers were in Spanish as she had made it perfectly clear that was her preference for the interview. Had this been the only interview in which this interesting dichotomy took place I would have chalked it up to the variety of quirks that is invariably a part of any research project. However, having gotten this answer once I needed to keep an ear out for similar responses. After all, it was still early in the trip and as I said before, I was willing to chalk it up to wrinkles in the Hispanic space-time continuum. What happened though, is that as I followed the same pattern of questions with everyone I spoke to, I kept getting very similar responses. Most of the Spanish-dominant or Spanish-leaning individuals I spoke to explained that yes, they did watch Spanish television the most, but that they also watched quite a bit of English-language television. When I pressed to get a sense of margin of preference what I got from a majority of the people I spoke with was always thin.

As we progressed through the major Hispanic markets I started to notice that when we were in these markets the people I spoke with tended to have a much wider margin of preference than in less-developed Hispanic markets. This did not really jibe with what I was thinking. I thought that in the more-developed Hispanic markets there would be more bilingual individuals—more people who watched balanced levels of Spanish and English television, which would, in turn, mean a smaller margin of difference in their preference. What I learned was the opposite and I had to find out why. The issue was figuring out some way of doing it. After some consideration I took the easy way out; I framed the issue and asked why.

What I heard made all the sense in the world and truth be told made me think, as my daughter says, "Duh!" The responses were as varied and eclectic as the people that provided them, but what they boil down to is this: Content. What the vast majority of people explained was that although the level of understanding of English clearly affected the television they watched, the content of what they watched weighed almost as much. So, for example, many people we spoke with watched *novelas* and news in Spanish, but like our lady friend from Mexico, they also watched *Desperate Housewives* and *Friends* and *ER*. As you can imagine, I had to get to the bottom of this so I asked the question you are probably formulating for yourself right now, "How is it that you say you function primarily in Spanish, but you watch these shows that are completely in English?"

> Although the level of understanding of English clearly affects the television people watch, the content of what they watch weighed almost as much.

And here we get back to the points I made when I started this chapter: Our assumptions about how language fluency and language of dominance correlate have been wrong and the way we define language use relative to advertising and marketing has been overly simplistic. You see, what I learned from these people is that while they function primarily in Spanish, they can receive information in both Spanish and English. Now clearly I am not a linguist and I do not claim this to be scientific or academic in nature, I am just relaying what I heard. Functioning, as you can imagine, involves both conveying and receiving information, while consuming media involves only receiving information. Spanish-dominant or Spanish-leaning people were decidedly more comfortable with getting information in English than with having to formulate and communicate ideas in English. Most explained that the process of learning English is much faster in the context of understanding than in the context of communicating. They begin to understand English way before they are able to communicate in English. In fact, many people that have been here for more than 20 years are still unable to speak English fluently, but understand more than 90 percent of what they hear.

Many people that have been here for more than 20 years are still unable to speak English fluently, but understand most of what they hear.

Now you can also see why there was a wider margin of preference in the more developed markets. There is more content available in-language and therefore more choices in-language. There are more television channels, more radio stations, more magazines, and newspapers available in-language. In less-developed markets there are fewer media choices, which means that if you do not want to watch the programs on the one Spanish-language TV station or listen to the music or programming on the two radio stations that come in garbled during the day only, then you have to tune into English-language television or radio.

We need to seriously reconsider the media consumption set even when we are talking about Spanish-dominant or leaning Hispanics. When we think about our target in relationship to categories, we can be more specific about who we want to talk to and market to. I want to make sure we do not fall into the trap of thinking that we can therefore assume that a 30-second television spot in English will have the same effect and influence as a Spanish-language spot. I can already see the grins and smiles of all the mainstream advertising professionals reading this and thinking, "I knew we were reaching them with what we are doing in English." Not so fast junior. They have been *exposed* to the ad. Thinking they have been *reached* by it is more wishful thinking than fact. We know from a number of independent studies—not sponsored by agencies or media companies—that advertising in Spanish to Spanish-dominant Hispanics is far more effective than English-language advertising for the obvious reason.

So now you are thinking, "So what is this guy saying? In one breath he is saying, 'Spanish-dominant Hispanics watch and listen to and understand English language programming' and in the next breath he is saying that 'You need to advertise in Spanish in order for them to understand and for the communication to have an impact.'" Are you really going to make me explain this? All right, but I'm only doing it because I didn't necessarily get it right away myself.

Let's Get in Their Shoes

I think the best way to do this is to frame it in a context that you, the reader, can identify with. Let's say that you are in France and trying to learn French. After six months to a year you have the basics down and are still learning every day. You watch the English-language channels available, but there are only reruns of really bad shows from the 1970s or CNN and you have cycled through the CNN headlines about 65 times already. So armed with your basic understanding of French you flip through the French channels and happen upon something of interest to you, whatever that may be. You sit and watch and are pretty happy with yourself because as you watch the show you understand more and more of what is happening. You see the characters develop, you see the context and the settings they function in and you relate it all to your understanding of French. Now, like television anywhere in the world there are commercials, in France they come at the beginning and end of programs. I am hoping that by now you can clearly see and understand the issue at hand. No? Well I'll spell it out. Watching and understanding and being affected by a 30- or 60-minute program is way different than trying to get the main idea of something that is flying at you in half a minute in a language you are trying to learn.

If you are thinking this is all great and entertaining, but what does it mean for me and my business, I agree and I am getting to it. What this all means is the following:

a. When we are thinking about what media we are going to run our Spanish-language advertising on, we can and should consider English-language media channels. True, not all will accept a Spanish ad on their network, but a lot will. In fact it is already happening. I am sure that many of you that are reading this book have seen advertising either all in Spanish or bilingual running on English-language networks. More media choices means better and more defined targeting and better results.

b. When you are developing your general market English-language advertising you should consider infusing some of it with culturally insightful elements. Even if the ad is not in Spanish, having truly insightful cultural cues will increase the impact on those Spanish individuals we were talking about earlier and will for sure capture and have an impact on your English and bilingual Hispanic customers, which will again, improve your bottom line.

c. As we consider a wider range of media choices and the programming we run our advertising with, we can also widen the portfolio of products or services we can market since some may make more sense marketed in English with some cultural cues added and others can be addressed through a stand-alone campaign.

d. There will most definitely need to be much better communication and cohesiveness between what you are doing in the general market and what you are doing in the Hispanic market both internally and between your agencies. "Silo" thinking is on its way out. Trust me on this one.

The other point I should make is that although it will most likely not affect your business in the short run, having and using a wider range of media vehicles will change the overall media landscape. The reason Spanish-language programming is what it is in the U.S. is that when it came to reaching Hispanic Spanish-language consumers it was the only game in town. As our friends from the road have taught us, it is clearly not the case anymore. As Spanish-language networks feel the pressure for better programming, they too will begin developing better and more varied programming. We are already beginning to see that in the development of shows that are much closer to what we see in the general market. We are also seeing the influx of networks and channels that broaden the choices Spanish-speaking consumers have.

Let me draw another parallel that you may be better able to relate to. Have you noticed what has happened with mainstream television and the quality of the programming? With the exception of one or two real dogs, the quality of network programming has drastically improved over the past few years. Shows like *The West Wing, 24*, and *Desperate Housewives* are all testament to an improved line-up across the board. Why did this happen? Did network executives all of a sudden say, "Hey, we should make less money and invest more into our quality of programming and production?" Are you kidding me? If these guys had their way and they weren't being forced to compete with the programming of cable and pay-service offerings, programs on Discovery, History, A&E, not to mention *The Sopranos, Sex and the City*, and *Queer as Folk* on HBO and Showtime respectively, they would be more than happy to get away with spending less and making more. The realization by the big four networks that they had better improve their offerings or face steadily declining ratings came with the growth and evolution of the "series" on pay channels and the improvement and proliferation of more specialized channels that offer programming targeted at a much narrower audience.

This should pretty well cover the whole language issue as it relates to media consumption. We will now move on to the issue of what it is we run on this wide range of media choices, another much talked about and debated subject. I think you will be surprised by what you hear.

The Death of the Acculturation Idea

Once again part of the reason that writing this is difficult and selling it to you is even more difficult is that we have been functioning under the wrong assumptions for so long. If you have considered marketing to or in any way communicating with Hispanics in the U.S. you have undoubtedly heard about acculturation.

Let's understand what acculturation is and what it is not. You may have also heard about assimilation and considered it to be synonymous with acculturation. That is incorrect. Let me explain why. Acculturation is the process through which an individual internalizes certain elements of a new culture and incorporates them into a pre-existing culture. This process takes place over time and varies from culture to culture and from location to location. It is a dynamic process; it flows, but the pre-existing culture remains.

Acculturation is the process through which an individual internalizes certain elements of a new culture and incorporates them into a pre-existing culture.

Assimilation, on the other hand, is a linear process. It involves the "shedding" of a culture and its replacement with another culture. This process continues from generation to generation until the pre-existing culture is all but completely gone. Both of these processes involve the acquisition of a culture so it is easy to see why there can be confusion.

When it comes to the Hispanic culture in the U.S., acculturation is the measure by which we determine who we should talk to when it comes to marketing or advertising. Obviously this is not the only or even the most profound use of acculturation, but for our purposes it is what we will refer to. So when we talk about, or consider communicating with, Hispanics in the U.S. what we have always done is to determine where in the acculturation process our target consumer is. Once again, the reason is that we have long assumed that there is a correlation between acculturation and language preference, awareness of brands of products, personal and family values, and other components present in all of us regardless of ethnicity. Obviously the better we understand these human definers the more effective we can be in communicating with our target audience.

The good news is that when it comes to language fluency we have not been incorrect in our assumption. Language preference does correlate pretty directly with acculturation. Less-acculturated Hispanic individuals do prefer to speak Spanish. The problem comes when we make absolute determinations about acculturation and we do not contextualize it across categories, across geographies, and across other non-Hispanic cultural considerations. If you are thinking to yourself, "What *is* this guy talking about?" hold your horses, I'll get there.

For those of you who have not done work with Hispanic consumers let me explain. When clients come to us "experts," what we have always done is to explain this whole acculturation thing in general terms. Given the correlation that we have already determined exists, we explained that when we talk about marketing to Hispanics in Spanish, it naturally flows that most of our consumers are in the less-acculturated set. They are still early in the acculturation process. So far, so good. Yet, once again, the thesis is turned over by those pesky people I spoke with on the road. As always, I think the best way to explain this is to put you in the picture with the people with whom I spoke and to try to let you into a composite of the actual conversations I had.

Picky Penny? (Speak in Spanish)*

After doing what I do for a while you begin to fall into certain patterns of behavior and it happened to me. Whenever I speak with

---

* "Picky penny" is what it sounds like in English when Spanish-dominant, low acculturation Hispanics try to say "speak in Spanish?" They usually mumble and speak quickly, so it sounds like they are saying "picky penny?"

Hispanic individuals in the context of marketing or advertising, I automatically try to determine where in the acculturation process they are and whether they are "acculturated" or "unacculturated." After all of the years doing this, it just happens. So as I spoke with every one of the Hispanic people I ran into, I instantly began the process of making this determination based on what I was hearing from them. And again, they proceeded to completely redefine my understanding of the idea of acculturation and how it is relevant to what we do.

Alicia and her sexual proclivities

So come along and sit and listen as I speak with Alicia in Phoenix. Alicia told us that she most definitely preferred to function in Spanish, but her job required her to function in English so as you can see she falls in the truly bilingual segment of the population. Right away I am leaning to the "acculturated" side of the equation. Remember the correlation between language dominance and acculturation? Well, here it is playing a critical role in how I am sizing up this woman. The conversation progressed and Alicia began to tell me about the way she lives her life, her value system, and how she considers herself, all very profound and significant elements of who she is as a woman. She explained that she has very deep ties to her culture, that she truly believes in a woman's role in the household, in the relationship between children and their parents regardless of how old you are, the warmth and emotive nature of the Hispanic culture, and her Mexican heritage, all of it spoken in English, but with a marked Spanish accent. So now I am reconsidering my assessment and I am beginning to lean back to the "unacculturated" end of the equation. I am thinking, "If I had to explain to a client where this woman falls I'd have to say that she is 'unacculturated' based on what she is telling me about herself."

This is no big deal in that it does happen that we can start going in one direction and come back to the other side once we get a better read on who we are speaking to. The significance of this conversation comes from what happened next. As we were talking, Alicia drifted very subtly and naturally into the realm of sexuality. As you can imagine I was a bit taken aback, given what she had just shared with me about her values and ideas.

The conversation progressed and she began to open up even more. She explained that she felt that one should be able to express one's sexuality in whatever way made the most sense and made you feel good. She said that sexually frustrated Hispanic women would never be able to realize their full potential because there would always be a part of them that yearned for something. I am relaying this to you, not to shock you with the nature of the content of the conversation, but rather to crystallize for you why I now once again needed to rethink how I was defining and why I was coming back to the "acculturated" end.

I don't want to belabor the point, so suffice it to say that as the conversation progressed this seesaw continued in my head. When we wrapped up and got back on the road I was a bit loopy from the conversation I had just had. This is where having the time and distance to think came in handy. I began to formulate an idea and to understand what I was hearing, but I didn't want to get ahead of myself, especially since this was based on one conversation. The fact that this happened, though, most definitely meant that I was going to be paying specific attention to this dynamic in my other conversations and I would try to probe around this idea as we went on. Sure enough, as I continued to have conversations with other Hispanics I noticed the same dynamic.

I'll let you in briefly on another conversation I had with a guy in Orange County. This conversation started off significantly different from the one I just shared with you. This gentleman was completely Spanish-dominant. I again went on autopilot and defined him as "unacculturated," although now armed with the insight I gained through conversations like the one with Alicia I was ready for the seesaw dynamic once again. Sure enough, it happened again. We started at the "unacculturated" end given his language preference and the fact that he had arrived in the U.S. just 18 months ago.

We happen to have a car company as a client and this guy happened to have an Audi so I steered the conversation in that direction. I thought I could get him to open up with something he was passionate about. And he did indeed. We talked about cars for almost 45 minutes. He had very detailed knowledge and understanding of the performance of a variety of cars. Although he had told us he only finished high school, he was very well versed on the engineering of European, American, and Japanese cars. So at the end of this conversation I thought to myself, "If I had to define this guy to my automotive client I would most definitely have to say he is in the 'acculturated' end of the equation."

After this and many other conversations that reflected this same dynamic I was ready to solidify and better define the idea I had while driving. I will now share it with you, if you haven't figured it out already that is. The idea and concept of acculturation as we now know it and use it is dead, kaput.

If you recall how we started this, you will remember that where we were headed was down the oversimplification path once again. We wanted a quick and convenient package to wrap our ideas around and we happened upon "acculturation" as a viable and supportable proposition for why we should talk to who we are talking to and why we should say what we are saying. Well, we now need to rethink it, not reinvent it or completely scrap it, but rather reframe it and figure out how we can use it more effectively. And I think our friends from the road may have provided us with a great start.

What I came to realize is that acculturation as we are now using it may be sending us down the wrong path. (I'll get deeper into this wrong path idea a bit later.) Acculturation without context is pretty useless and yet the first thing we do is to define our target based on acculturation and then get into the context of it. *We need to flip that*. Before we ever think about, talk about, and use acculturation we need to look at many other factors, not the least of which is the category we are going to be marketing.

Let's take Alicia from our earlier conversation and see how we would have defined her now and how we would define her if we were to indeed flip this thing upside down. Alicia is bilingual; she functions primarily in English given her job requirements, although she does consume some Spanish television. She is a college graduate, a professional in an executive position, which in turn affords her higher income. Based on these factors I would say the vast majority of those of us who work on this for a living would define her as an "acculturated" Hispanic. We would then look at our category, product, or brand and decide if our target would be "acculturated" Hispanics or "unacculturated" Hispanics. If we happen to decide that our target is primarily "unacculturated" Hispanics then our friend Alicia would most likely not be a part of our considered customer set when deciding who we will talk to and what we will say. Now you see the problem.

What we should do instead is to always contextualize our assessment of acculturation with the specific category, product, and, if possible, brand we are going to be working with. We need to do that *before* we decide on messaging and what we should be saying. Let's also take our automotive friend from Orange County and see where he would fall out. This one is actually pretty easy because, as we have now said a couple of times, language dominance does correlate with acculturation. So given our friend's most decidedly Spanish preference we would determine he is "unacculturated." After making this assessments certain assumptions would automatically flow that would determine our messaging and whether we need to consider our friend in making that determination. In the most obvious example the following would likely follow from the determination that he is "unacculturated":

> He would most likely think favorably about American brands and models. Larger sedans would play well with him. Status is important to him, but price also plays a critical role. Value

in the automotive category to this individual is most likely defined by the combination of the price for the status the brand offers.

As we begin the process of developing our messaging to address our target you can see that if our target is "unacculturated" the above thoughts should be considered and we can begin to formulate the seeds of ideas. But we also know that the individual we spoke with on the road and who would fall under the "unacculturated" definition under our old thinking is actually very "acculturated" when it comes to the automotive category. He is primarily performance driven. His idea of value would most likely be the performance, not the status you get for the money that you pay. So messaging around the idea of status for the money you get would most likely not be too compelling for our young friend.

Now I know that you are probably thinking, "Is this guy kidding? Of course we are all different, but you have to generalize in order to define a viable target segment, you can't target individuals." Agreed, completely agreed.

My point here is to say that when we are following a process for developing that segment we need to rethink how we use "acculturation." So far, our thinking has not given us what I would call a truly successful model. I think the additional advantage to first analyzing the category, product, and brand cycle is that we can better synchronize to the overall, general-market strategy, which as we will see is critical to success in marketing to Hispanics in the U.S.

Portraits

Rolando Peralta
Age 25, Miami, Florida

My name is Rolando Peralta and I am from Cali, Colombia. See, I bet the first reaction you had to me telling you I was from Colombia was something to do with drugs. I don't know what you thought exactly, but if it had to do with drugs, specifically cocaine; deny it, I dare you! Then when you heard Cali, Colombia it was like, oh for sure this guy had something to do with drugs and you probably started thinking about Harrison Ford blowing up crap and playing the big anti-drug, American hero. Let's see you deny that too!

Don't worry, it's not just you, it's pretty much what I get no matter who I am with or where we are. Obviously people don't say anything, but you can absolutely tell they are thinking something along those lines. Maybe it would also help for you to know that I am 25 years old. I dress pretty nice and I like to frequent nice establishments. Oh now you can see why! Well, actually I can too, which is why when people ask I say I am from other cities around Colombia and not Cali. Actually I had a friend who had it worse. His name was actually Pablo Escobar and he really was from Medellîn, can you believe that? That's like saying your name is Adolf and you really are from Germany; it flat out sucks. Although I do have to say we have used it to get a few laughs, especially with girls we meet who have no clue that Pablo Escobar has been dead now for a few years. I can't tell you how many times we heard, "Aren't you afraid of getting put in jail just walking around here in Orlando?" The funny thing was that as they

---

Portraits presented here are composites of people I interviewed on my trip. None is intended to represent a particular person.

were asking this they had a certain glint to their eye and they had begun to get cozy. We would let the illusion play out until we had to leave and the valet pulled up in Mr. Escobar's exotic 1995 Honda Civic. I actually told the girl I was with that he drives that to stay undercover; his other car is a Ferrari. The amazing thing in all of this is that they believe us!

Back to my situation. My parents sent me here to go to college and I went to the University of Miami. I met a lot of other guys and girls from Latin America who were here to get their college education. Actually, to me Miami didn't really feel any different than home. Most people spoke Spanish and the whole feel of the town is very Latino, but I guess that's to be expected with as many Cubans as live there. Anyway I came here to go to college and the idea was that I would go back to Colombia when I was finished and get a job there. It was a nice idea, actually more of a dream, because there is just nothing to go back to in Colombia. It's sad but it is the truth; there are no jobs to be had for young professionals coming out of school. So what I have decided to do is to get my MBA and to get a job here in the U.S. I'm not quite sure that I will be staying here forever, but I sure know I will be here for at least the next ten years and then who knows, maybe I meet someone and I get married.

I will tell you that one of the biggest surprises to me has been my discovery of many Colombian groups here in the U.S. since I've been here. To be honest I always expected to find Cuban or Mexican or Puerto Rican groups because those are the largest populations, but going on the internet I found a bunch of groups made up of people from Colombia. The thing that surprised me the most is that some of the biggest groups seem to be in North Carolina. North Carolina? Now there is something I really wouldn't have thought about, but it's true. I guess once some people from a country in Latin America get to a destination it stands to reason that they will tell other people from that country about it and they in turn will follow. I myself am thinking of going out there and checking it out, seeing what it is like and seeing if I can meet any of my people.

As far as my every day routine goes, it's pretty normal. I get up, go to work as the manager of a clothing store in a mall here in Miami and then in the evening I go to classes for my MBA. Yes, I do party a couple of times a week, alright, 3 or 4 times a week, but *koño*, how else are you supposed to meet girls in this country? When I'm not working or going to school or partying I watch some TV. I have TiVo so the shows I can't watch because I am at work or whatever I just record. The ones I record the most are *Desperate Housewives*, soccer from Mexico, *The Sopranos* when it is on and *Smallville*. Now that I think about it, about the only thing I watch regularly in Spanish is Mexican soccer and that's because there is no broadcast of Colombian soccer. I do check around though because sometimes ESPN en Español or Fox Sports might have highlights or scores for teams back home.

I have tried to watch some of the Spanish language channels, but it is clear to me that they are definitely going for a different audience. I still can't figure out why, on the Spanish news, when there is a significant event or happening they are reporting on, they go out and interview the lowest common denominator they can find. No offense, I know it's their audience and everything, but come on, what do you think you are going to get when you ask someone who clearly just got off the bus what they think about today's horrible tragedy? When I see stuff like that I get disappointed and I change the channel.

Radio is a different story though. I listen to the radio a lot, at work, on my way to work, at home—both English and Spanish and some in between. The music has gotten really good regardless of the language, which is what I would hope will happen with TV, that they will come up with better content, regardless of language.

Things are actually getting pretty rough back home and my dad keeps telling me not to worry, but I know better. I am worried about my younger brothers and my sister and to be honest with you once I finish my schooling the only reason for me to go back would be my family, but if I can get a good enough job and make enough money I think I am going to try to bring them here rather than go back myself.

Sometimes people ask what the difference is between Colombians and other people from Latin America, say Guatemalans, Mexicans, etc. When people ask that, I think to myself that there is not much of a difference, but then as I start to answer I realize that there is. Even though there certainly is economic instability in those countries as well, those of us that come from Colombia have, I think, over time developed a bit of a thicker skin when it comes to the cruelty that life sometimes has in store for us. We take it more in stride. It's not that we condone it or have gotten used to it as many people think, and even less that we have begun to rely on the drug trade as the way to support our families, although for many families it is the only way. For most, it's not any of those things; I think we have just come to realize that there is only so much we can do with what we have and in the situations we find ourselves in and I think that kind of mental peace gives us a more cool demeanor when we get hit hard by something. Now please don't talk to me about generalities, alright?

I am a college student and I know I can't speak so broadly, but I am talking about my opinion of some of the biggest differences between Colombians and other Hispanics. Anyway, in case you didn't know this Colombian Spanish is the Spanish most often used in the U.S. when translating materials, did you know that? It is the most neutral Spanish there is. Although truthfully it really does depend on where you come from in Colombia. I think I hear my friend honking outside, we are going to a Shakira concert. You didn't think we would miss her when she came to town did you? How many other Colombians have made it as far as she has? More importantly, how many other Colombians look like that and can sing and move like that? I rest my case.

5

Who Cares Why They Came?

W HEN WE THINK ABOUT marketing to U.S. Hispanics we take into account a host of considerations in order to communicate effectively with our audience. The one thing that we almost *never* take into account is the *why*. *Why* did the people that came here actually come here? Please don't come up with "Because they were looking for a better life." That is obvious. Of course they were looking for a better life; we all are. I can tell you that every morning when I get up I am looking for a better life.

What I mean is what were the actual motivators, the principal drivers for people coming to the U.S.? There will always be the overlay of a better standard of living and a better overall life when we talk about the reasons people come here. But there are also other, very profound reasons for people coming her. If we really want to understand the Hispanic population we need to revisit some of those issues that brought a lot of us here. We are not going to retrace the travels of Amerigo Vespucci here, but we will go back to the 1970s and come forward.

The 1970s and early 1980s

In the 1970s and 1980s, socialism and communism were very much alive and thriving in many of the countries of Latin America. El Salvador, Chile, Guatemala, Honduras, Argentina, among others had political unrest based primarily on the enormous gap that existed between the haves and the have-nots. There were many other political and historical reasons for the unrest, but at its core, the economic gap drove the unrest. As a result of this unrest there was a violent manifestation of loyalty to one side or the other that evolved into a war, declared or not—a war that had caught many innocent people in its midst. Anastasio Somoza, the Sandinista movement, *Sendero Luminoso* (Shining Path), and Augusto Pinochet are all party to a violent and sad era that was a part of Latin America's social evolution in the 1970s and 1980s.

As you can imagine, for many of the innocent people caught in the middle, these events lit a fire to leave the country they loved. So relative to what we are talking about in this book, most of the people that immigrated to the U.S. during this period had something other than just socioeconomic reasons for leaving. Many families came here as a result of persecution, whether actual or perceived, by one of the sides in the conflict.

Many families came here as a result of persecution.

During this era, the Mariel boatlift also took place. For those of you who are too young to remember, the Mariel boatlift was the largest single migration from Cuba to the U.S. to this day. In 1980, Fidel Castro responded to growing pressure from the U.S. and accusations from the international community that he was a ruthless tyrant by allowing Cubans whom he found "undesirable" to come to the U.S. or go anywhere else they chose. These undesirables were Cubans he considered to be unpatriotic and a threat to the ideal of the motherland. They were often brilliant thinkers that supported free thought, free trade, individual freedom—things that are threats to all deluded dictators. Miami was the destination most of these people had in mind, if for no other reason than its geographic proximity. However, Fidel also thought he would take advantage of this social "purging" to get rid of a huge number of real criminals and socially and mentally deficient individuals by sending them to the U.S. along with everyone else. So, the vibrant and rich culture that is most definitely a critical part of the Miami we know today was shaped by the individuals that came in the

Mariel boatlift. Unfortunately, that holds true on both the positive and negative sides of the culture.

Why is all of this important when we think about marketing to the U.S. Hispanic market? Well, the quick answer to that is mindset. The mindset of these individuals was to a large extent driven by the fact that they were leaving their countries of origin, not necessarily because they wanted to or even because they were driven to do so by fear for themselves and their families. This mindset, however, as it would be for most of us, was also infused with an element of hope—hope that at some point the situation in their home countries would be settled and they would be able to go back home.

Why is it important for what we are talking about? Because it may help us understand that when it comes to some products and services such as investments, mortgages, and home improvements, their underdevelopment among Hispanics has nothing to do with the consumers' inability to acquire or try to acquire some of these things, but rather with the fact that they were thinking, "This is just temporary. Eventually I will go back." With that mentality, you can see pretty clearly that regardless of how much we market to them about long-term investments in the U.S. it will be a tough sell, no matter what their socioeconomic or educational level.

If you are saying, "What's so different about the social and political conditions in Latin America now? There's still instability and a huge gap between haves and have nots," you're right. It's true; those conditions still exist. However, we all know the fall of communism and changing economic dynamics have changed the way in which people in those societies deal with the political situations they face. Most obvious is the fact that there is significantly less politically driven violence. We are all keenly aware that narcotics' trafficking has continued to make violence a harsh reality in many of these countries. However, for our purposes, we can determine that the violence spawned by that activity is clearly illegal and universally condemned by the international community. Therefore it is not perceived or considered by the population as a possibility for how their country will eventually end up. And that makes all the difference when it comes to mindset, which as I said at the beginning, is what is important when you are considering how to communicate with them in a meaningful way.

The 1990s: Show Me the Money

If the 1970s and 1980s were about social and political instability and its effects on various populations, the 1990s were all about the money. Let's accept the fact that everyone coming to the U.S. envisions a better way of life and a higher living standard and both of those things have to do with money. In the 1990s the U.S. was coming out of a recession and experiencing economic growth. Coupled with that, there were devaluations in many countries, most significantly in Mexico, which in essence meant that if you had money in the bank, all of a sudden it was worth half as much in the international market. If you were a professional in your home country, let's say Mexico, the idea of making twice as much money as you were held true appeal. To make it crystal clear, in the early 1990s, if you were an engineer in Mexico, making what by local standards was a pretty decent wage, you would most likely not be thinking of when you were going to move to the U.S. Then, let's say that the Mexican peso devalued by half, that previously you had to pay $5 pesos for each dollar you bought and now you had to pay $10.

When there are devaluations, one of the most significant economic consequences is that in order to keep the money in the local banks and from leaving the country, banks raise their interest rates to ridiculously high levels, which also means they have to raise those rates when it came to the money they lend. It doesn't take a math genius to see that no matter what your profession, if you earned money in dollars, you would overnight be making twice as many pesos. The trip to the U.S. becomes a lot more attractive then

> Let's accept the fact that everyone coming to the U.S. envisions a better way of life and a higher living standard and both of those things have to do with money.

and the most tangible way to significantly increase what you make. After speaking with many Mexicans, I have found this to be true especially of the white-collar workforce that ended up coming here even if it meant accepting a job well below their educational levels. Once again the significance of this for us is mindset. Although the motivations for it were different, the mindset is the same.

People were coming here to make money and send it back. Given the exchange rate, their money would go much further back home. The key here is the "back home" part. Again the stay here was temporary. Once they had built the house (in Mexico) or bought the ranch, they would be going back home. Again those categories that would require an interest in long-term planning would be a pretty difficult sell. They were here only temporarily, even though in many instances they had been here for more than ten years. Mindset, remember, mindset.

Things were about to change forever. The most significant change in the early 1990s was the adoption of NAFTA (North American Free Trade Agreement). Basically the passage of NAFTA signified the opening of the borders between Mexico and the U.S. from a commercial standpoint. The agreement meant that Mexican manufacturers and businesses would have an easier time exporting their products to the U.S. However, more important for our discussion it also meant that U.S. companies would have a much easier time bringing their products or brands to the Mexican marketplace.

A Mexican today has been exposed to and is familiar with myriad different categories, products, and brands that they would not have had access to as late as 1993.

Why is that significant to us here in the U.S.? What does it matter given that we are talking about the Mexican marketplace and what we want to do is sell to them in the U.S.?

It means that when we talk about a recent arrival, I mean really recent, like two days in the U.S., a Mexican today has been exposed to and is familiar with myriad different categories, products, and brands that they would not have had access to as late as 1993. So when we, the "experts," tell you that you have to educate the consumer you need to take it in context and with a huge grain of salt. Some of it may be true, but a big part of it could be some of the "self-preservation" grandstanding that we are given to from time to time. This coupled with the emergence and evolution of global communications definitely will cause a fundamental shift in the migration mindset we have been talking about, a shift that has a tremendous impact in how we market to Hispanics in the United States.

The 21st-Century Home Sweet Home

Now we come to where all this has led. This will bring the idea of migration rationale home for you and make it clear why not considering it may prevent your initiative from achieving its potential. The principal difference between immigrants in the late 20th century and today is that now the U.S. is a completely different world for the immigrant than what it used to be. We considered some of the things that were a part of the impetus for coming here from the immigrants' perspectives, but what happened on this side that has fundamentally changed things?

Well, we come back to the 1999 Grammy Awards and the Cup of Life. The 2000 census numbers, economic stagnation, and the end of the dot-com bubble all combined to focus attention on the Hispanic market across the U.S. and throughout corporate America. Suddenly being Mexican, Colombian, Puerto Rican, or Cuban was the in thing to be, and the Hispanic market became the new business frontier. With this new interest and the realization of the financial and political value of the U.S. Hispanic population, the U.S. became a much friendlier place for Hispanics. We now know that this is indeed a fundamental shift and not just some sort of fad. Multiculturalism is not only accepted, but also embraced across the U.S. Even the most homogenous communities are seeing a shift in the make up of their population.

The result is that now the U.S. is the principal destination for what I would call a socio-cultural migration—a migration in which individuals come here with the *mindset* that they are here to stay. They are thinking about investing because they are thinking about what their lives will be like when they are age 65 and retiring from their jobs here. They are looking into mortgages and home ownership because the money they had been sending back home to build a house or buy land is now going to bring the rest of the family here.

The U.S. is now the principal destination for what I would call a socio-cultural migration—a migration in which individuals come here with the mindset that they are here to stay.

How does it affect how we communicate with U.S. Hispanics? When you think about your future, the idea that you will be here for the rest of your life ignites a desire to own a house, to invest, to plan for the long-term, which opens up a number of categories that were previously underdeveloped.

Given current world events, the U.S. is taking a much more focused and prominent position in keeping illegal immigrants from entering the country. While the stricter enforcement is meant to apply to all illegal immigrants, we know that by virtue of geography it will affect immigrants from Latin America the most.

The problem is that the fundamental shift in mindset I have just described applies equally to Hispanics who are already here as well as those who remain in their countries of origin. Along with the change in enforcement there is a more significant and deeper shift in the mentality of the Hispanic illegal immigrant. It is the difference in thinking about the U.S. as just a place that you come to make more money and thinking of the U.S. as the place that you and your future generations will call *Home*. It is the difference between trying to keep someone out because it is your job and someone figuring out a way to get in because it is their future.

How committed are people about coming into the U.S.? In 2003, 19 immigrants died while locked in the back of a trailer with no air on their way from Harlingen to Houston. Approximately one hour into the trip, a point at which some of them were already going into heat-induced shock, and maybe dying, they went through a checkpoint and they chose to remain quiet. They were locked in those conditions and they *chose* to remain quiet. Does that give you an idea of how much it means to many people to come here? Compare that with the commitment of the Minutemen—those vigilantes guarding the borders in Arizona.

6

Being Human before Being Hispanic

MOST HISPANIC AGENCIES have a hard time getting senior management's ear to talk about Hispanic marketing for another reason: When we come through a new or prospective client's door, the first thing we do is tell them why their campaigns for the general market are completely ineffective when it comes to Hispanic consumers. We tell them why they have to come up with something completely different. Believe it or not, one of the most significant conclusions I have come to over the years is that most of the truly effective programs targeting Hispanic consumers are based on fundamental, human ideas—ideas that have nothing to do with the fact that the target audience happens to be Hispanic.

When it comes to marketing, I think we can agree that the more consistent the message, the more impact it is likely to have. This is particularly true when we are talking about the essence of a brand and what it stands for. A brand should be appealing and relevant regardless of the audience. Ultimately it must try to appeal to a human aspect.

So, for example, when we are talking about alcoholic spirits we can agree about certain things that are true of all of us, regardless of where we come from. Alcohol reduces inhibitions so we become more social creatures; we tend to consume alcohol in high-stakes social situations; and we want what we drink to reflect positively on us. Would you agree this is all true? If you do, then you can see that when it comes to spirits there are many things about all of us as human beings that could be leveraged to develop an effective communications program. In fact, it is precisely these things that are most likely the basis for what a company does to capture the general market. If all of this is true—if we are indeed all human before Hispanic and it is those things that make us human that companies base their mainstream advertising on—then doesn't it sound a bit self-serving and shortsighted to have Hispanic marketers saying that what is being done in the general market is useless?

I can tell you that based on many conversations with executives and potential clients, it sure sounds self-serving to them. And even if we forget about the self-serving aspect of it, we could be walking away from the key to our own success in marketing to Hispanic consumers. I can tell you that right or wrong, at Cultura, we look first at the general market efforts. We try to see what they are based on from a brand standpoint, from a competitive standpoint, and from a human standpoint. Not until we have looked at all of that and conducted a thorough analysis of it do we move on to looking at it from a Hispanic perspective.

For us it is actually pretty simple: Remember Occam's Razor? We take a look at what you are doing successfully in marketing to the general market. We then see how far it could take you marketing to Hispanics and if it falls short, we are there to take it the rest of the way. Over time, this has proven to be the most effective way to earn credibility for our efforts and the most effective way to begin to have access to senior management. Telling a prospective client, "This is what you are doing right." is better than saying, "This is wrong; you have to do something different." Imagine if your girlfriend said that to you. It doesn't feel great does it?

Of course, there will be occasions when the client really should be considering the Hispanic market from a different perspective. When those instances come, if you have taken a more human approach in coming to that conclusion, you have a much more viable proposition to sell.

Taking a more human approach also makes us more valuable at the strategic table when it comes to the general market. Most of those sessions need as many good strategic thinkers as they can get. Approaching it this way makes us a valuable commodity—bilingual, bicultural marketing professionals willing to put the health of the brand and the success of the campaign before our own Hispanic expertise. Sure we can walk through the door with the old standby, "That won't work; we need to do it differently." However, we take the risk that at many levels of the organization including senior management, the thinking will be, "Oh, boy let's hear what we've done wrong now and how much it will cost to fix it."

The bottom line here is that those things that are true of all of us as humans can and should provide us with a very solid position from which to launch our Hispanic efforts and that the insights about all of us as humans are most likely a part of the general market initiative. Just throw the whole self-preservation theme out the window and go get what you need without having to reinvent the wheel. I think your clients, your employees, and most important, your consumers will be most impressed.

How Hispanic Should it Be?

This is one of the most-often-asked questions from an advertiser perspective. From an agency perspective, it is one of the most important aspects of what we do. Unfortunately, it is the question that we most often get wrong as agencies and experts. The reasons are wide and varied. Suffice it to say that the principal reason we get it wrong has a lot to do with the self-preservation dynamic I mention throughout this book. The most accepted response to this question is that the less acculturated, more Spanish-dominant the consumer, the more we need to infuse the commercial with authentic and culturally relevant elements. In other words, the less acculturated the consumer, the more Hispanic and more authentic the commercial needs to be. This sounds perfectly logical right? I mean, the more recently arrived, the more the consumer will yearn to see and hear things with which they can identify.

The problem with this whole dynamic is that it is flat out wrong. The principal reason for this error has to do with the difference between a consumer finding something interesting, relevant, or familiar, and making it have an impact on his life. There is a subtle difference, but it is a critical difference and one that should shape the communications targeting the U.S. Hispanic consumer.

You may be wondering how I came to this little epiphany. It actually happened in a pretty pragmatic way. Throughout my career, I have had the opportunity to be a part of many research projects and studies. As you can imagine many of these studies had to do with testing advertising and marketing campaigns among Hispanic consumers, something that makes complete sense when you are planning on investing significant dollars in producing a spot or launching a campaign. So we would go out, recruit the respondents or participants in the study, test the concepts, and wait for the answers. And we would get the answers we liked. Hispanic consumers would go into great detail about why they liked the commercial or concept we were testing. We would hear answers like, "It reminds me of home." or "I really like it; that is what my family is like." and we would be pleased. We would go back to our dens and we would move forward producing the spot, or launching the campaign, or executing the event, or whatever else we happened to be testing.

Then we would test the program or spot for effectiveness and *we would get flat results*, regardless of the measure we were looking for: brand awareness, sales, leads, or something else. This happened over and over again and being a researcher and, most of all, a curious marketer I wanted to know why this was happening. We seemed to be doing everything right, so why weren't we getting the results we wanted? At this point I should clarify that these commercials, campaigns, and research studies took place while I was working with a number of Hispanic agencies and with a number of advertisers directly, so it's not like we could say that this happened only with agencies or just in instances in which companies were marketing directly to the consumer. In this regard we were all equally confounded. Back to the story. So what was the deal; why was this happening?

In this type of situation, when something is not making sense the thing to do is to trace it back step by step and figure out where the issue is. What I ended up with was the fact that while we might be doing the right thing by testing, it was almost impossible to test for the thing that mattered most—impact. We could definitely find out if the target consumers liked the program or commercial and we could find out if they thought it was something they could relate to. However, as I found out, liking it and thinking it was something they could relate to did not equal impact and, ultimately, results. After a while I decided to do some side research while we were out testing these programs. I would, when possible, take some alternative options and ask some questions on my own. What I found was a bit surprising, but the more I thought about it, the more sense it made. I have to warn you that what I am about to share with you is going to sound counterintuitive to some and flat out crazy to most. However, it definitely reflects the difference between having consumers like what you are doing and having an impact on consumers in a way that actually sells your brand, product or service.

> *Hispanic consumers on the un-acculturated end of the scale are more likely to be persuaded by commercials that incorporate contemporary and aspirational elements reflecting the at-large popular culture in the U.S. than by commercials that incorporate authentic Hispanic cultural elements.*

What I found was that we had it completely backwards. Hispanic consumers on the un-acculturated end of the scale were more likely to be persuaded by commercials that incorporated contemporary and aspirational elements reflecting the at-large popular culture in the U.S. than by commercials that incorporated authentic Hispanic cultural elements. On the other hand, more-acculturated Hispanic consumers (the ones we think are most probably addressed by English-language advertising rather than by Hispanic, Spanish-language advertising) are far more persuaded by culturally charged and targeted advertising.

Let me repeat all of this once again since I think you are probably sitting there saying, "Is he saying what I think he's saying?" Yes I am. Advertising that reflects the at-large popular culture in the U.S. has more of an impact on Hispanics who are recent arrivals and that are otherwise considered less acculturated, Spanish-dominant consumers. Culturally charged advertising that reflects Hispanic culture has more of an impact on those consumers who are more acculturated or English-preferred.

To confirm what you are probably thinking, we did have it completely backwards. As I told you earlier, it was a bit surprising, but only until I thought about it for a minute. Then it made perfect sense.

Let's take a step back and analyze the forces at play here. You have a group of foreign-born Hispanics who have come to the U.S. looking for something. Whatever that something may be, most of these individuals have gone through significant efforts to get here. For some it is truly a life and death journey while for others it is a matter of time and money. Any way we see it, it is a journey that exacts a cost and a journey driven by ideas and hopes. So we have this group of people that come here looking for new ideas, new people, and new experiences, all as part of a larger dream.

Once people get here they begin the process of acculturation. They begin to realize some of the ideas and hopes they came looking for. While they are undergoing this process we decide we will communicate with them. We brilliantly come up with the idea that since they are just recently arrived or un-acculturated, we should address them by putting in front of them those things they have just come a long way to change. It's not that these consumers are getting away from their culture, but they most want to become a part of another culture. Once we understand this dynamic, some of what I have shared with you probably becomes clearer. No? All right let's try it another way.

The idea of what the Hispanic market is has remained pretty constant for well over a decade. You know exactly what I mean. Even if you haven't done anything to reach the Hispanic market you have heard "the formula": Hispanics are family oriented; Hispanic women take care of their families; Hispanics love their music; Hispanics go to the supermarket as a family because it is a family outing, and so on. We will get into what is true and what isn't true a bit later on in the book. For now, let's just take it in the sense that this model, the one outlined above is the one that *everyone* works from and I will give you a guess as to what that means. You're right! The work that comes as a result ends up looking very similar. It's not that it is bad work. A lot of it is actually very creative. Unfortunately even the creative work ends up looking similar to other creative work. The work accurately reflects the culture. All of this is great if that is the purpose for doing it, but alas it is not. Impact and results are the measures of success when we think about Hispanic advertising.

Given the combination I just outlined, it is not difficult to understand why Hispanic consumers are attracted to more contemporary and aspirational advertising. They see basically the same type of advertising in Spanish—advertising where everyone uses the same cultural model to communicate. In spite of being culturally charged and authentic in reflecting country of origin, this advertising is the equivalent of wallpaper to the target consumer. They like it; they recognize it, but after a while it just blends into the background.

If you are back to thinking that this must mean that you just need to translate what you are doing in English to reach the unacculturated U.S. Hispanic market effectively, hold your horses because you'd be making a huge mistake. In my experience, the most effective advertising targeting U.S. Hispanic consumers is heavily infused with popular culture, ideas, and elements that are appealing from a *human* standpoint laced with some cultural nuances, when appropriate. In most instances subtleties that clearly communicate a deep understanding of not only the culture, but also the acculturation dynamic we have just gone through have the most impact.

On the flip side of this, well crafted, culturally charged commercials, whether they are in Spanish or English have more impact on the acculturated, English-dominant, or bilingual Hispanic. This also makes sense, once you think about it. We are over-marketed as general market consumers. We see the widest and most imaginative work every single day, so much so that we get numbed to it. So if, while we are in the middle of this process in which we are drowned in advertising, we suddenly see something that incorporates our culture—a culture we are now hungry to see reflected properly and in a compelling way—we stop and watch and we remember who did it. This is even more pronounced when the advertising is developed in English and run on mainstream television. In that instance we literally stop to watch and listen.

As a matter of fact, some of the most impassioned and committed responses come from Hispanics watching Spanish-language advertising on English-language mainstream television. This is true of both acculturated and un-acculturated Hispanics alike. And while the reasons they give for this are varied, what I have been able to ascertain is that this advertising provides a sense of validation as individuals and as a culture. For less-acculturated Hispanics it provides a sense that they are being taken seriously and for more-acculturated Hispanics it feels like we are being considered as a part of the mainstream culture, also providing a sense of validation. In my opinion, understanding this dynamic will make the difference between good Hispanic advertising agencies and great Hispanic advertising agencies.

The key here is to realize that while we may be getting the right answers, we might not be asking the right questions and that we should shape those questions around the one thing that should matter most, results.

Portraits

Maricela Uribe
Age 28, Charlotte, North Carolina

My name is Maricela Uribe and I am half Puerto Rican, half Venezuelan, although I consider myself Puerto Rican. I have been in the U.S. for 18 years. I have a bachelor's and an MBA and I am an executive at a financial services company. Actually I am in charge of Hispanic marketing for the company. I have been doing that for the past 5 years. The reason I was put in charge of Hispanic marketing is because I am Hispanic. It doesn't take a genius to figure that out. I know the Hispanic market in the U.S. I know the cultural aspects. I know their shopping and buying behavior. I know everything I need to know to market to them. How do I know? Didn't I tell you I am Hispanic? What else do you need to know?

Because of my job I have to present an image of success and assertiveness so I like to wear only designer outfits and use designer handbags. You know what I mean, Prada, Roberto Cavalli, and Gucci, that kind of thing. As a young professional Hispanic woman I need to make sure to make a statement. I watch all of the fashion shows and read all of the fashion magazines for that reason. I read the magazines' English versions most of the time because I think they have more recent or fresh fashions than the Spanish versions. I don't have anything that has given me that idea; I just feel that way.

I watch mostly English language television for my own consumption, but I have to watch Spanish language television

---

Portraits presented here are composites of people I interviewed on my trip. None is intended to represent a particular person.

because of my job. I can't think of any program on Spanish television that attracts my attention. I do listen to some Spanish-
language radio, but very little.

My husband does construction work so you can tell I definitely did not marry him for his money. That's for sure. He is
from Venezuela and does not have a college education, so it is
mostly my income that supports us. So now you must be
wondering how it is I can afford all of the name-brand things I
mentioned earlier. I guess it won't hurt to tell you. They aren't
real; they are just replicas, very good replicas, but replicas still.
I can't pay $2,000 for a purse, are you crazy? But I do need the
caché, so I have to do it. See, the trick is to know what people
look at when they are trying to spot a fake—I mean a replica.
Once you know what that is, then you can go and get a replica
that meets all of the requirements of the original. Also, you can't
just go to New York and buy the fake crap they have there; you
have to know where to get it and you have to be ready to pay
top dollar. A good Prada replica should set you back at least a
couple of hundred dollars.

We don't have any children yet, but we will try at some point.
Right now I am too focused on my career and don't really have
the time to have children. I work with a lot of companies in my
job, some good and some bad, but the advantage is that, like I
said, I know the Hispanic market. The agencies I work with
know that, and they know they need to make sure they come
up with work that I will approve of. I truly have no interest in
working with partners that think they know better or think they
can change the flow of what we are doing. No way I want to
fight with the companies I work with. The reality is that since
I know what I am doing it is my way or the highway. Like I said
at the beginning, I am a professional Hispanic woman and I
have to assert myself.

My parents still live in New York; my mother stays at home
and my father is a building engineer. I love my parents for every-

thing they have done for me, putting me through school and giving me everything you could think of, but I promised myself I would not be like my mother when I grew up. She is very traditional in her beliefs about what a woman's role is and she never pursued anything professionally although she had many interests. I also remember that my father was very hard on her and her perspective that sometimes a wife just has to put up with some things. That included him cheating on her. So maybe that's why I am so driven and why I tend to take the lead between my husband and me. I just never wanted to fall into the same thing she fell into. Sometimes I wish I hadn't gone through those things because obviously they affected me and sometimes I do wonder what it would be like to have a more traditional perspective. Sometimes, especially when I see my friends with their kids I do get a little bit jealous. And sometimes I also get a bit jealous when I see their husbands being a bit more assertive and taking charge more. I wonder what it would feel like to be taken care of more. Oh well I guess for now I'll just have to settle for the office, the expense account, and the feeling of being in charge.

7

Grassroots, Events, Community Outreach . . . Oh My!

T HIS IS A TOPIC that has confused the overall purpose of each of the elements that are outlined. It is one of those topics that rubs me the wrong way, if for no other reason than we are misusing these organizations and events. So I think the best thing we could do is to come up with the correct definition of each and the way that it should be used in the context of Hispanic marketing. I hope to be able to do this because after many conversations with clients and colleagues alike it has become clear to me that there are many in our industry that are seriously confused about what each is meant to do.

Let us start with **grassroots efforts** because they are mentioned most often. To begin with, grassroots is defined as initiatives that are *initiated and executed by the members of a community or group belonging to the community.* So when we are talking about grassroots we have to understand that the consumers we seek to target have to be a part of the team that executes the initiative, whatever the initiative may be. They need to be the on-the-ground element that diffuses the message or helps you to make a connection.

Let's get a bit more real-life because I don't want any confusion about this. It is amusing to listen to some companies talk about their grassroots initiatives. You know the ones, where they have trucks going out to the community handing out products to consumers. That's their grassroots program, or what they think is a grassroots program. In this case, though, not a single member of the community or group associated with the community is involved in executing any part of the program. The true grassroots initiative is the one that begins exactly in the place that we want to reach—the community. It is community generated and executed and it is the best example of the opportunities we are looking for.

> The true grass-roots initiative is the one that begins exactly in the place that we want to reach—the community.

Let's say there is a soccer tournament that has been taking place in a community for three years and that the tournament has grown over that time based on the interest from surrounding communities. Let us further say that because of this growth, the original host community no longer has sufficient fields to host the tournament. This is a perfect grassroots opportunity. It is an opportunity for a company to come in and facilitate the improvement of those fields through financial assistance and personnel involvement if possible. In the end this type of effort is still owned by the community and that given the corporate interest will continue to be. And it is an instance in which a brand involved itself in a way that made sense and that made a difference. In short, the brand made a connection with the consumers in that community and because it is the community that owns the initiative it will be the community that will also carry that brand message from mouth to mouth.

I had the fortune to observe this with a league in Los Angeles. I was meeting with league directors because a major sports label wanted to form a bond with Hispanic soccer players in unaffiliated leagues. So we had a meeting with the directors of the league and at the end of the meeting I happened to look over and see a whole stack of Budweiser signs. I also saw that their lineup sheets and scoring sheets had the Budweiser logo on them. Naturally I asked them whether Budweiser was sponsoring the league. He told me that they were not. He explained that Budweiser had provided the signage and the advertising sheets for a tournament. The league directors liked how signs looked around the field so they used them every Sunday, and they just copied the sheets with the logo because, once again, it made the league look good. So here we have a company that got involved with the league when they had a need and then left them on their own and it was the league that continued to carry the brand. That is a grassroots effort.

I think this shows what it is we need to do if we are thinking about using grassroots as part of our initiative. We have to make sure the community is involved in its execution, not just in its consumption. When it is just consumption we are interested in then we are talking about an event, which we will get into a bit later.

Given what I saw while I was on the road, it seems to me that the best way to come up with a successful grassroots program is to figure out what is already happening in a community and in what way you could get involved. Sometimes an opportunity may come for a company to spark a grassroots initiative, but usually the most successful programs are those that originate in the community and then are helped along by a brand. Also key is listening to these community organizations when they tell you what they need, even when it is not how you were thinking of supporting them.

In the example above, the sports apparel company went into the initiative wanting to refurbish the community's soccer fields, but what we learned from the community was that they needed uniforms and soccer balls. It took a lot of doing to persuade the company to get involved in a way that the organization had expressly told them they needed. If the corporation had pursued its original idea of refurbishing the soccer fields, it would have been inefficient, and, at worst, counterproductive.

Events

An **event** is defined as an occurrence, especially one that is particularly significant, interesting, exciting, or unusual. It is usually an organized occasion such as a social function or sports competition.

Clearly the context in which we are considering events is marketing. Events as we know them are opportunities for a brand interested in the U.S. Hispanic market to meet the consumer face to face. Specialty firms that put an event together and then sell it to interested companies organize most events. The problem with today's ready-made events is that they are marketed to everybody, so if you really want to make a splash and build a connection you need to invest the money to do it up big or come up with something truly different. Otherwise you will get drowned out in the noise that every other marketer is there to make. The other key thing is to understand that being at an event does not necessarily qualify as community outreach. It only qualifies as community outreach if you are bringing something you have ascertained the community needs, and that you are now willing to provide. I get frustrated hearing companies talk about their community outreach efforts because they had a booth at a Cinco de Mayo festival. That's not community outreach. It's a great opportunity to meet people and have some authentic Mexican food if it's the right festival.

> *If you really want to make a splash and build a connection you need to do it up big or come up with something truly different.*

Community Outreach

Let us now move to the trickiest of the three, **community outreach,** community involvement, or community relations. For our purposes, I am going to refer to it as community outreach. Because it is sometimes confused with some of the other elements we just went over, the expectations are often misguided. Community outreach is defined as the relationship among different cultural, ethnic, political, or religious groups who live in an area and may come into conflict. It may involve mediation among these different groups who live in an area. Community outreach clearly has a political and social element to it. That being the case, companies in the U.S. usually get involved in community outreach through organizations whose charter is to deal precisely with those types of issues in the areas of interest. This involvement is usually through contributions or presence at events sponsored by these organizations.

In the Hispanic realm, The National Council of La Raza (NCLR) is a perfect example. NCLR does great work in addressing many political and social issues that are of concern within the Hispanic community and being involved with them is a great way for a company to show its concern for the community. However, getting involved with these organizations *is not* a marketing initiative. I believe that many companies in the U.S. get involved with organizations like NCLR with the expectation that they are going to see some kind of return on investment based on their involvement. What ends up happening is that since the initiative is not a marketing initiative the return on investment (ROI) is not there and the support wanes.

Unfortunately, because the promise of ROI is one of the principal reasons for corporate involvement, some of these organizations have begun to make some claims in that regard. I think this is unfair to the organizations, and it is unfair to the marketers interested in supporting them. The work they do is wonderful and over the long run, with some ongoing commitment and appropriate public-relations support these investments can yield positive results for the brand, but that is a far cry from expecting that community involvement is a marketing initiative. As I said, it is unfair all the way around.

It is clear that there is some overlap among many of these things. Some events can have a community outreach component and some community-relations organizations can put together programs designed as marketing programs. Key to understanding this and to using it effectively is to understand what each of these components is designed and meant to do and what it is not meant to do. Throwing it all together into one large bucket is a sure way to get confused and to perhaps tap into something that won't meet your expectations. Also key is to understand what community-based organizations stand for and what becoming involved with them will entail and deliver for your company. From my perspective, supporting community-based organizations should be considered part of any company's public or corporate involvement, not as a part of the marketing program.

8

Perceptions and Realities

S O FAR, I HAVE RELAYED to you in basic terms what I heard when I was on the road. With the exception of a few editorial peccadilloes, I have pretty much kept it straight from the consumer's mouth, but you didn't really think I was going to drive more than 10,000 miles around the country and not have a little something to say that comes just from me did you? I paid my dues and I think I have earned the privilege of sharing some of my ideas with you. Whether you agree is an entirely different proposition.

I have had the privilege of seeing and experiencing a culture grow, change, and ultimately define itself over the past 25 years. I consider myself to be particularly lucky because I had the opportunity to do so from many different perspectives. I saw it as a child trying to adjust to a new way of life; as a teenager trying to understand how, or even if, my heritage would contribute significantly to my self-identity; as a young adult trying to understand where in the context of the culture I fit and how that would affect my life; as a part of the blue collar labor force that toils day in and day out in garages, fields, and houses to make a better life for themselves; as a father trying to figure out what elements of the culture would and should be passed on to my children and trying to figure out how I was going to do that; and as a husband trying to reconcile the cultural values instilled in me since I was a child with my wife's view of that culture and a culture of her own. I truly believe it was that range of experiences that prepared me for my career and helped me decide what I would be doing for the rest of my life.

During the last 15 of those 25 years I embarked on a more focused journey. As I matured both personally and professionally, I have been fascinated by how the Hispanic culture is defined, communicated, and ultimately perceived in the United States. I have chosen to make my living by bringing two cultures closer together and trying to have perception reflect, as closely as possible, the reality of who the U.S. Hispanic is. While I do this principally in a business context, I can tell you it has been impossible for me to keep it only in that context.

In the last few years, the chasm between what the culture is versus how it is perceived by the population at large has not narrowed as much as I would have thought it might. Everything that has happened in the past 10 years—9/11, the internet, the unbelievable advances in telecommunications and global media technology—has transformed pop culture in the United States. Yet if you analyze how the perception of the Hispanic culture has evolved over that time, you can see that today's Hispanic culture in the U.S. sounds and feels a lot like the Hispanic culture of 10 years ago.

Please notice that I am saying it *sounds* and *feels* like 10 years ago. In reality, the Hispanic culture that has evolved is quite different than it was 10 years ago, and that evolution is speeding up. I accept that gaps in how something is perceived versus how it is are a part of the human experience. I think we are always trying to narrow those gaps, but deep down we all know they will always be there. It is part of the magic and fun of watching life unfold and always being surprised by some aspect of it.

What frustrates me about this particular picture has little to do with the natural gap that will always exist. My frustration stems from a deep conviction that one reason for the huge gap between how the Hispanic culture is perceived and what it has become is our desire to be able to readily package and sell it. In my opinion, the reason such a discrepancy exists today has everything to do with those of us who make our living by trying to help the rest of America understand the U.S. Hispanic culture. I include all of us in the Hispanic marketing arena in this group. However, there are a lot of other folks who have contributed just as much. I include politicians, clergy, medical professionals, contractors, lawyers, academicians, and activists. In fact I think academics and activists along with those of us in marketing communications and the media have done more to stagnate the evolution of the popular perception of our culture than anything else.

Obviously the implication of such a disparity between perception and reality filters across almost every aspect of life, but for the purposes of this book I will try to stay within the realm of marketing.

Am I saying that those of you who are not part of the U.S. Hispanic culture and don't make a living understanding it don't know the real U.S. Hispanic culture? Am I saying that while it is clear that the U.S. Hispanic culture has changed dramatically in the last 5 or 10 years, in parallel with the at-large U.S. popular culture, your perception of the culture does not reflect that change? Am I really going as far as saying all of that? Yes, I am saying exactly that. All of the information I have shared with you in this book speaks exactly to that point.

The gap between perception and reality is definitely not in the business value of the U.S. Hispanic market.

The gap between perception and reality is definitely *not* in the business value of the U.S. Hispanic market. The market really is as big an opportunity as people believe it to be. In fact, it is precisely that increase in interest that has brought most of these issues to light.

The actual gap between perception and reality comes in the process of developing an understanding of the culture in order to market to it. Like any other consumer segment successful marketing to Hispanics hinges on truly understanding who Hispanics are as people. Like it or not, it is the human aspect that drives and defines consumer behavior and there are certain universal elements true of all humans, not just Hispanics. And that is where we get in trouble. Somewhere along the line we have forgotten this and have made being Hispanic more important than being human.

First, let's recognize the fact that when we say Hispanics we are not talking about a *race*, we are talking about *ethnicity*. This makes total sense when you look at the U.S. census figures, which include a significant percentage of people who may define themselves racially as being African American but ethnically as Hispanic. Suffice it to say that ethnicity does not equal race. (Why is this important? Let me tell you, I have almost been arrested for throwing a fit over a police officer putting down that I am Hispanic when it comes to race. You know what I mean; you get the ticket with all of your information filled in and when you see race filled in as Hispanic you have a huge fit. Oh, you haven't had to go through that? The officer cannot understand what it is you are so indignant about —especially in L.A.— and you just won't give in.)

Probably the most dominant perception of the Hispanic market is that it is Spanish-language driven. This is the case even though by now most people know that the U.S. Hispanic population is roughly 50 percent bilingual and English-dominant and 50 percent Spanish-dominant. People think only in terms of Spanish because they believe that since English-speaking Hispanics can understand English-language communications they are being reached effectively by those communications and thus nothing needs to be done. English-speaking Hispanics are, from a business standpoint, considered to be mainstream consumers. I believe this is shortsighted and, in fact, counter-intuitive from a purely business standpoint, but I will not belabor the point. Suffice it to say that, as I have mentioned elsewhere in this book just because people understand something it does not mean they are being addressed in a meaningful way.

Geographic Segments

PERCEPTION: The Hispanic population is composed of three primary ethnic segments—Mexican from the Midwest to the West Coast, Puerto Rican in New York, and Cuban in Miami.

REALITY: The Hispanic population in the U.S. is made up principally of people from three countries: Mexico, Puerto Rico, and

Cuba. The population in the U.S., as you might have already gleaned, is becoming more diverse with people coming from a variety of cultures and with more combinations of the people that are already here. It is no different with the Hispanic population. Central and South Americans are becoming more prominent across many of the fastest-growing Hispanic markets in the United States. During my visits to North Carolina, for example, I noticed a significant Colombian population that seems to be growing weekly and seems to be driving a significant part of the growth of the Hispanic population in the area. Also, the largest Argentine population outside of Argentina lives in Miami.

Although there is a strong geographical correlation between countries of origin and the area in the U.S. where people end up, that is also changing. It still holds true that Mexicans make up most of the population in the Midwest and Southwest, that Puerto Ricans and Dominicans make up a significant part of the population in New York, and Cubans make up pretty much all of Miami, but these distributions are most definitely changing.

Central and South Americans are coming into Miami in record numbers. Economic instability, a Hispanic-friendly environment, and the fact that many significant companies use Miami as a staging area for Central and South America fuel this immigration. Given the rate of influx of Central and South Americans it will be interesting to see how the population in Miami shapes up in the next five years. Don't get me wrong. Miami will always be a Cuban culture through and through, but I am interested in seeing how the size of the various nationalities evolves.

Mexicans will always be the largest of all Hispanic cultures in the United States. Currently the Mexican-Hispanic population makes up anywhere from 65 to 75 percent of the overall Hispanic population. The reasons for this are based on geography and logistics more than anything else. No matter how much time passes, traveling 800 miles to cross a border will *always* be easier than traveling 3000 miles. The Mexican culture, from a population numbers standpoint, will always be number one. From the standpoint of household and disposable income, I believe Cubans will be number one for a long time to come. Mexicans are the fastest-growing segment of the Hispanic population in New York so it will be interesting to see how Mexicans relate to the Puerto Rican and Dominican cultures so well entrenched in New York.

In all of the conversations I have had with people from these cultures some pretty consistent characteristics have emerged. These include the deferential nature of the Mexican and the Central American and the brashness and outspoken qualities of the Puerto Rican, Cuban, and South American cultures. When it comes to the Caribbean cultures, I think it is their free entrance and flow from the U.S. to their home countries that emboldens them and it is the harsh and difficult journey that most Mexicans and Central Americans have had to endure that makes them a bit more reserved and a bit more deferential. Coming back from being deported is not as easy as jumping on a plane. There are monetary and human costs that are paid in order to come here, so anything considered to increase the risk, including stating opinions is likely to be avoided.

Cubans, Puerto Ricans, and most of the Caribbean cultures do in fact love Salsa, the dance, and are very good at it, but that is not the whole story. Of all the things I have said in this book, it is this next one that I believe will actually generate death threats, but I can't lie. I will tell you the truth and if the threats come, well, *asi viene el sandwich*. In my experience and judgment, the best Salsa dancers I have seen have been either Colombian or Venezuelan. I will soften the blow to my Puerto Rican brothers and sisters by saying that in many instances the couples I spoke and partied with were made up of a Puerto Rican or part Puerto Rican. I think the reason for this is that Salsa in Puerto Rico is a bit more staid and traditional while, at least based on what I am told, in Venezuela the variety of Salsa played and danced to is more contemporary, which means that as Salsa dancers Venezuelans have to be more adaptable and flexible in how they choreograph their moves. I will also say that of all Hispanic cultures, the Venezuelan culture is the most similar to the Puerto Rican culture, right down to the accent. If you are thinking I am still going to get some threats, I wholeheartedly agree with you. All of this is meant to say if you are thinking Salsa, Puerto Rican or Caribbean, think again.

Physical Characteristics

PERCEPTION: Physically Hispanics tend to be shorter than Anglos, darker-skinned and have dark hair. Men generally have some facial hair.

REALITY: The general physical type that we associate with the Hispanic population is indeed darker skinned. (I am dark-skinned and have Mexican and Puerto Rican tattooed on my forehead.) Hispanics come in all shapes and sizes, from very dark-skinned Afro Hispanic in appearance, to mocha-toned mulattos to very light-skinned, light-eyed, light-haired Hispanics. There are also, as you probably already know, some beautiful combinations of all of the above.

As you try to communicate effectively with this consumer you would be well served to remember this little tidbit. If you are at this very moment remembering some focus group or another in which you heard un-acculturated Hispanics saying, "They need to have more Hispanics in the ad," referring to darker-skinned, darker-eyed, and darker-haired individuals, please get it out of your head. In all of my experience I have yet to hear a Hispanic that is not in a forced, socially awkward situation, like that of a focus group for example, say, "That is just not for me because the people are too light-skinned." It hasn't happened and I guarantee you it will not happen when someone sitting in his or her living room watches the commercial, especially if it is infused with culturally relevant nuances.

Culture

PERCEPTION: Hispanics love music, mostly Salsa.

REALITY: Hispanics do love music and in particular salsa. In study after study, conversation after conversation it was Salsa that was the common denominator among Hispanics of all backgrounds. So if you want to ask people whether they like Salsa and leave it at that, then great. However, if you are considering what music to use in your initiative and you are considering Salsa, press the eject button immediately, pull on the emergency brake, or the rip cord, take your pick, but please think it over!

What's so wrong with Salsa? Absolutely nothing, if all you want is something to use behind your great creative. If you want to generate an impact and actually make a difference you might want to consider any of the other types of music that Hispanics also like: Mariachi, Banda, Duranguense, Bachata, Cumbia, Norteño, Reggaeton (which is picking up some serious momentum, and is exactly what it sounds like, a Spanish version of the Afro-caribbean rhythm we have all come to know and love), Rock en Español, hip-hop, jazz, R&B, oldies, pop-balladas and so on. Get the idea?

The problem with Salsa is not that people won't like it or will respond negatively to it. The problem is that everyone and his sister has been using it as the de facto choice in music when it comes to U.S. Hispanic consumers. Frankly a great deal of the advertising that has used it has been, and continues to be, some of the cheesiest and most horrible around. (Watch any 10-10 commercial on Spanish-language TV and see if I'm lying.) Overall, though, I do have to say that music if used properly can be one of the most effective elements in Hispanic advertising. Volkswagen's and Heineken's use of popular songs from Latin America with incredibly relevant lyrics are perfect examples of the effective use of music by Hispanic advertising agencies.

PERCEPTION: Hispanics love spicy food; they put salsa on basically everything. Hispanics love salsa any way they can get it.

REALITY: Hispanics do indeed love spicy food, but not all Hispanics. Hispanics from countries with a European heritage like more seasoned food, but not necessarily spicy food.

The relationship between the hot pepper and the cultures of Latin America is historically undeniable so it would stand to reason that many of the native dishes from our countries of origin contain or are seasoned with hot peppers. As generations have gone by, however, the definition of what is hot and what isn't varies significantly. By the way, thus far I have found absolutely no correlation between level of acculturation and the resistance threshold for how hot something is. I have watched both acculturated and un-acculturated Hispanics hit jars of *jalapeños*, as well as the more fiery *chile de arbol* (tree chile) and *habaneros* and not flinch.

Salsa is now the most consumed condiment in the U.S., surpassing catsup as the condiment of choice. The permutations of what salsa is are wide and varied in look and taste. The more garden variety, the kind you have most likely tried at some point if you have gone to a Mexican or Tex-Mex restaurant, generally speaking contains tomatoes, cilantro, onions and *jalapeños* in some combination. Most of the time this concoction looks green, red and white depending on the amount of each of the aforementioned ingredients.

I think some Hispanics have gotten tired of the fact that the same word is used for the music Salsa and the eating salsa and have come up with *Pico de Gallo* to refer to the eating kind. It is this garden variety of salsa that I am claiming is the same as *Pico de Gallo*. I have yet to find a significant difference between what constitutes *Pico de Gallo* and salsa. Personally what I have experienced is that salsa is what most of the at-large population uses and *Pico de Gallo* is most often found on restaurant menus. Salsa to a Hispanic though, principally a Mexican Hispanic, looks and tastes very different than it might to you. Salsa includes green salsa, *habanero* salsa, *chile de arbol* salsa, cream-based salsa, *chile guajillo*–based salsa, each of which looks and tastes different from the others.

PERCEPTION: Hispanics love their cars, decorating them in a variety of colorful materials, religious icons or those frilly hanging things with the little balls on the window. Oh, yeah and let's not forget the all-important baby shoe hanging on the mirror. (When I was 17 I asked my dad to hang up one of my soccer cleats on the mirror of his car. He didn't think it was funny. He also didn't think it was funny when I hung one of his soccer cleats on my mom's mirror; she didn't think it was funny either). Of course if you are a younger Hispanic you also need to think about really low, small rims even when you own a truck (in some places, especially if you own a truck), small steering wheels that look like a chain, and last, but definitely not least, a hydraulic system for at least one of the axles of the car. (If you really want to be able to make the thing dance you definitely need it on both axles.) Religious figurines on the dashboard are also an important decorating item, even if you yourself are not so religious. Placement of religious icons is optional. You can put them on the dashboard or you can have them painted somewhere on the car. The *Virgen De Guadalupe* is always a safe choice, although your own personal saint also works.

REALITY: Yes, we love our cars, but there is more to the story. We love our cars because along with clothing and jewelry we believe the car is one of the most significant ways of communicating one's station in life.

Although some of us in the more acculturated end of the spectrum would like to think that it is really the un-acculturated that place badge value or status in their cars, we have to face the reality that it is just not the case. Regardless of acculturation or socioeconomic level, the automobile does play a more significant role among Hispanics than among non-Hispanic whites. The other reality is that while it may be more marked among Hispanics, the idea of the car as a social icon is certainly not unique to Hispanics.

The social aspect is often the reason for the decorations on some Hispanics' cars. Religion and the belief of protection by one's saint is a significant part of the motivation for decoration in whatever form it takes. (A quick digression to explain what I mean by one's own saint. In the Catholic religion you can basically find a saint with your name no matter what your name is. A specific day is dedicated to each saint, and when that day comes you get to celebrate almost as if it were your birthday. I was born on December 28, three days after Christmas and three days before New Year's. My saint's day, thank the stars, is June 24, day of San Juan.)

Religious icons are not the only inspiration for decorating cars. Girlfriends, mothers, lost friends all can serve as inspiration for how someone might decorate his ride. Overall, acculturation correlates somewhat with how much a car is adorned, but not as much as you would think. If you talk to the people that are really into the decoration of their cars—the low profile rims, the hydraulic kits, and the chain steering wheels—you quickly realize that it is mainly English-speaking Hispanics who have the most radical rides.

By the way, the cost of customizing some of these cars is more than the average yearly salary. In my opportunities to see these cars and talk to their owners, some had put more than $100,000 into their cars. So while the amount of decoration on the car is indeed a good indicator of the background and possibly the socioeconomic level of the decorator, it would be foolish to over-assume what it means and how to use it if at all.

Hispanics also love performance and high-end cars. Hispanics in many countries in Latin America have as much access to high-end brands as we do in the United States. Obviously high-end brands are costly, but they play a prominent role in marketing to drivers in their country of origin. In the case of Mexico, the residents actually have access to *more* brands than we do in the United States. In Mexico you can buy every brand you can buy in the U.S. plus brands like Seat and Renault. You can also buy different models of familiar brands. My point is that the days of the wide-eyed Hispanic who comes to the U.S. to encounter brands he has previously only read about are over. Access to those brands is easier in the U.S. and therefore the brand takes on a different aura, but the wonderment that used to be there seems to have turned into more of a 'tell me more' type of attitude.

Today customization of cars is also shifting along the same lines that the general population is seeing. Modifications that are meant to improve a car's performance and handling and, in some instances, actually turn it into a race car are becoming more prevalent. I am also beginning to notice an interesting combination through which some racers, after realizing their car will never be the fastest, have begun to spend to modify it along more traditional "Low Rider" style, which is the more aesthetically-driven style that I described above.

Hispanics are and will continue to be a receptive audience to the automotive category, particularly those brands that speak to Hispanics in a way that has an impact. When it comes to cars, impact comes in a lot of colors and shapes. While some of these considerations might feel awkward from a purely "politically correct" standpoint they are there to be considered nonetheless.

PERCEPTION: Hispanics love soccer or baseball, depending on where they come from. If they are Caribbean, they love baseball. If they are from anywhere else they love soccer. Most people know that Caribbean Hispanics love baseball because practically half of Major League Baseball players are from the Dominican Republic, Puerto Rico, or Cuba. A significant number of people know about these countries only because their favorite player comes from there and even then they know very little. Think I'm exaggerating? I had an assistant brand manager from Chicago ask me once if the Dominican Republic was in South or Central America. I told him it was between Argentina and Peru. He said, "Oh, yeah . . ."

REALITY: Hispanics do in fact love soccer, some with an intensity that only a fan in the U.S. would be able to understand. So yes, soccer is as popular among Hispanics as you think it is, perhaps more. And yes, baseball is as popular as you think it is in Caribbean countries. You don't think that the fact that more than a third of Major League Baseball players are of Caribbean Hispanic descent is just a happy coincidence do you?

The problem is that in the process of using these sports to appeal to consumers, we have numbed them to our efforts. Advertisers know soccer is popular and therefore use it in their commercials, most of the time in a very traditional and staid way. Same thing with baseball, although its popularity among the general population and the fact that more than 70 percent of the U.S. population comes from somewhere other than the Caribbean puts baseball in a bit of a different category.

When it comes to Hispanics and sports, the biggest point is that most people think that the Hispanic sports horizon opens up when foreign-born Hispanics come to the U.S. What I have found is the complete opposite. In our countries of origin, there is a diverse and vibrant sports environment that goes beyond soccer and baseball. The fact that we choose to ignore it in the U.S. does not mean that it does not exist in the countries we come from. In fact, the way I see it, we are being smacked in the face with this very significant idea.

Can you think of a Latino in the NBA that was a major figure in San Antonio's winning the NBA championship? Have you heard the accent and the level of English proficiency of many of the skateboarders and in-line skaters in the X Games? Do they sound a bit Portuguese to you? They do to me. Have you checked out where many of the top breakers for surfing in the Americas are located? You didn't really think the young men and women who *live there* just sat it out did you?

My point here is that if we are looking for meaningful communication with U.S. Hispanic consumers the time has come for us to employ every relevant angle we possibly can and when it comes to sports that angle should consider something other than soccer or baseball. Even if you insist on using soccer and baseball, how about using them in a way that breaks the mold? What if you were to think about soccer in the context of Hispanic women and sports instead of just males and only in the way they are used to seeing it? What if you were to start a female soccer league or organize a female baseball game?

Again, soccer and baseball are one way of reaching the U.S. Hispanic market, but the way in which they are being used now in advertising is, for the most part, ineffective. More participation and less observation will always be most effective. Hispanics, regardless of age continue to play both baseball and soccer so what if you were to address the older Hispanic population with a soccer or baseball program in which they could participate? See the idea? If we do not get ahead of this, I can guarantee you that the environment and the way that sports naturally evolve within culture are going to force us to consider other possibilities. With an MVP candidate in the NBA and two new Mexican drivers, Adrian Fernandez and Michel Jourdain joining the NASCAR Busch series it is not difficult to see that it may be happening already.

PERCEPTION: Hispanics are incredibly jealous and great lovers.

REALITY: While I can only attest to the latter point personally, I can confirm the former based on third party conversations. Hispanics are very jealous for the most part. When I asked people about jealousy, I got, as you can imagine, many different answers. However, one thing became clear to me. It had as much to do with perceived cultural propriety as it did with being insecure about your mate or any of the other reasons we might think of here in the United States. In fact, when questioned further, the majority of people were concerned with their mate's flirtations and behavior because of what other people might think more than because of what it means to their relationship. This was particularly marked with Hispanic males. They were significantly more concerned with how they would be perceived by their peers if their women were behaving inappropriately. Behaving inappropriately ranged from leaving the house without them to hopping on the back of a Harley and coming back three hours later smelling of booze.

PERCEPTION: Hispanics love bright colors, mostly primary colors in everything they can get them on, especially *serapes*.

REALITY: Half of this statement is true, we do love bright colors, mainly primary colors, but it depends on what they are on and what it will be used for.

In all the time I have spent understanding the market I can tell you that I have found that Hispanics are much more open to using brighter, more vibrant colors on everything from house decorations to clothing to the paint on our cars. How bright and how much depends as much on individual taste as it does on acculturation, so while there is some correlation between how acculturated you are and how open you are to using bright colors, it is not a direct or even dominating correlation.

The use of bright colors is not an attribute limited to the Hispanic culture. Serapes just happen to be one of the more ubiquitous elements of Hispanic iconography and one that is used quite a bit in the United States. Some Hispanics, particularly in New Mexico and Phoenix, Arizona brought up the connection between these colors and icons and the Native American and cowboy culture.

Whereas I think it is a mistake to use bright colors and traditional visuals in advertising without regard to how or when it is done, I also think it is a mistake to shy away from using them for fear of being stereotypical and offensive. As with several of the points I have made, this is where you need a truly insightful partner to help you navigate.

Women

PERCEPTION: Hispanic women are still comfortable filling a very defined and traditional gender role within the household. They take enormous pride in making food from scratch and feeling like they are really taking care of their families. Hispanic women, therefore, are somewhat adverse to instant or pre-prepared food products.

REALITY: Hispanic women are indeed comfortable with their role of caretakers within the household. Ideally they would love to make meals from scratch every time they cook, but they don't.

Based on visits to many Hispanic households, I believe that Hispanic women actually feel more comfortable with gender roles because, unlike in their countries of origin, they do not feel limited by that role here in the United States. It's not that they are a part of the Women's Lib movement or anything of the kind. It is simply that they understand that in most instances the U.S. middle class requires two incomes to sustain a household, which means their role will be expanded from the culturally driven definition of a homemaker. These women, however, require flexibility in order to maintain their roles within their households and still bring money home.

According to the U.S. Department of Commerce, Hispanic women are the fastest-growing entrepreneurial segment in the United States. It makes sense doesn't it? They need to be able to dictate their hours and have flexibility in order to maintain both of their roles. Likewise, that is why they have absolutely no problem with instant or prepared food. Once again, if you remember hearing Hispanic moms in a focus group saying, "I make everything from scratch," get it out of your head. What else are they going to say in front of ten other moms they do not know? Do you really think they will admit that at home their freezer is replete with frozen foods and their pantry is filled with canned food?

PERCEPTION: Hispanic women are more reserved and traditional than non-Hispanic white females. This applies across age ranges. Speaking about sex and about intimate issues is inappropriate and, in fact, taboo among Hispanic women. Homosexuality is still a sensitive issue among most Hispanics.

REALITY: Overall, the subject of sexual and intimate issues, including homosexuality, is more sensitive among Hispanics. Although this hesitation to speak or acknowledge many of these issues is rooted in religious beliefs and customs, there is also a purely social component to it. Most of the people I spoke with were succinct and clear, if not helpful, in their answers. "You don't talk about it because you are not supposed to talk about it," is the composite of the answer I got most often.

Attitudes about sexuality do, however, correlate with the amount of time foreign-born Hispanics have spent in the U.S. The interesting thing is that those attitudes correlate both ways. The longer someone is in the U.S. the more open and free they feel to talk about issues *and* the longer someone spends in the U.S., particularly when that someone is a parent, the more they believe they need to be cautious and prudent in how they raise the children and therefore become more closed and strict about enforcement. So while there is a correlation, it is not as straightforward and one-directional as we might think.

Another aspect of sexuality among Hispanics is that while the aura of the old school, old-fashioned more traditional Hispanic cultural values still permeates the topic, it doesn't completely rule it. More and more Hispanic women, not just the more acculturated or third and fourth generations, are willing to discuss, argue about, try to understand, and deal with issues of sexuality. More openness about sexual issues has come to Latin America as it has to the rest of the world, by necessity. With the spread of HIV/AIDS, governments in Latin America realized (some too late) that there would have to be a more concerted effort to inform young people and to encourage discussion of these issues.

Notice I said inform and discuss, not discourage. You see, while abstinence may be the rule according to the church, for the government safe sex became a much more viable proposition. Most governments knew already that sex outside of marriage was taking place. Now they just had to make sure that when it was taking place it was taking place in a safe manner. This means that recently arrived women have most likely had some exposure to information on safe sex and pregnancy, regardless of marital status.

Although Hispanic women are most definitely more reserved about having a conversation about sex, they are becoming much more open to talking about it, particularly to a friend or relative. In many instances women that were asked about their ideas relative to discussion of this topic answered that whether they discussed it or not depended a great deal on the situation and the company they were in. So the problem wasn't *if* they would talk about it, but rather *where* and *with whom* they would talk about it. If we as marketers are able to provide the right *where* and the right *with whom*, we will be much more successful in addressing the issue, whether it is from a public policy or a commercial standpoint. Hispanic women across the full spectrum of acculturation are becoming more open to discussing the idea of birth control, especially since many of the pharmaceutical and medical organizations and companies are offering more information and choices.

The one issue that really does still remain quite taboo in the Hispanic culture it is the issue of homosexuality. Hispanic gays are significant in numbers both in the U.S. and Latin America.

They parallel the overall gay population here in the U.S. in that their households tend to be better off financially and they tend to have more disposable income. Most of the gay Hispanics I spoke with were very acculturated. What this correlation tells me is that acculturated Hispanics are more willing to talk about and openly discuss their sexual preference and that less-acculturated Hispanics are more hesitant to discuss it openly, usually for social or religious reasons.

In the end, from a marketing standpoint, the Hispanic gay community in the U.S. is a vibrant and unaddressed group of consumers that could turn into loyal consumers if someone were to recognize them and address them. If you think that it would be good enough to address them from a gay perspective, you are right for the most part. Most of the gay Hispanics I spoke with told me that they identify themselves as homosexual first and then Hispanic, relatively speaking. All of them, however, were intensely proud of their culture, perhaps more so than the at-large population. If you are considering an initiative to capture the gay community in the U.S. why not address this component of it in a way that may help you make them loyal customers for life?

PERCEPTION: Hispanic moms are masters at making their children feel guilty about not taking care of them or not calling or coming by enough.

REALITY: If you are Hispanic and you do move out of your parents' house and begin a life, you can pretty much guarantee an expectation that you will call, come by to visit, or send something on a consistent basis. If you do not, you will be considered an ingrate and will be accused of being like a crow that has come down to take your mother's or father's eyes out. This last bit is on the more dramatic end, but a healthy dose of guilt if you don't call or come by is a very strong possibility. The crow thing is really there quite a bit in one form or another. I had a chance to speak with many other fellow ingrates about it and they've heard it too. I'm sorry, but I had to make reference to the *cria cuervos y te sacaran los ojos* so beloved by many Hispanic moms, at least by mine. If you are a Hispanic Jew the guilt thing with mom becomes a statistical certainty. One of my best friends is Jewish and his mom is a master at the guilt thing. He falls for it every time, even though he is with her almost all the time!

In the U.S. the distance that many immigrants have come also heightens this guilt. For many of them this is the first time they are living outside of their parents' house. This is a transition that is difficult for many of us that have grown up and lived here in the U.S., so I cannot begin to imagine how difficult it must be for people who are dealing with it as recent arrivals in a new world. The incredible thing for me is the fact that this is something I surmised from my conversations with people, but it was never brought up by anyone I spoke with as something he or she would have to overcome.

Most foreign-born Hispanics mention missing their family—not something unique to Hispanics—but other than that they never said, "I have to get used to living on my own, without my family." In retrospect it is easy to see, given this dynamic, why they might feel more comfortable living with a lot of other people. I think that although they do not articulate it or mention it specifically, they recognize that for many of them this is the only family they will be seeing for a while.

You will need to consider these issues and dynamics when you are thinking about what the Hispanic household looks and sounds like if you want to come up with something that has impact. Obviously it is not required that you use a Hispanic household in your communications. I am just saying that if you are, there is much more to consider than the neat little picture of the traditional nuclear family that seems to make its way into every Hispanic ad in the universe.

Families and Households

PERCEPTION: Hispanic households in the U.S. include the extended family, which really means that they can have up to 17 people living in a single room.

REALITY: Many Hispanics live in dwellings too small for the number of people living in them. The reason for this is simple. People live in cramped quarters to save money. Most of the time they send that money back to bring their family here, or help build a house, or pay for someone's operation. Some do it simply to save money. In other instances as the family grows, the house or apartment they live in gets smaller, particularly when you include the family, which when it comes to Hispanics can mean a third cousin twice removed.

What also does not get mentioned is that regardless of the number of people or the size of the dwelling, in most instances the place is incredibly neat. People take care of it and clean it, even when it is just males living in the household. When I had a chance to go into some of these dwellings the only way to tell there was a large number of people living there was by the quantity of food in the refrigerator or pantry. Some of these guys actually made schedules for cleaning and keeping the place up so sometimes these places were neater than your average house. If I had a choice between living in some of the houses I have seen with one or two people living in them (e.g. houses with cars on blocks out front and weeds in the front yard) and a two bedroom apartment with nine other Hispanic guys like the ones I had a chance to speak with, I'll take the nine roommates any day.

This brings me to another relevant dynamic within the Hispanic household. Part of the reason for a high number of Hispanics living in cramped quarters is that the family grows. This means that as the family grows people don't leave to make way for new arrivals, visitors, or newborns. We tend to stay in our parents' home until we are much older than the at-large population. I write this with no fear of offending or upsetting Hispanics because the same stigma that comes with this situation in the U.S. popular culture does not exist in the Hispanic household.

Whether it is because we are going to school, or just got married and are saving up for a house or simply do not yet have anywhere else to go, Hispanic sons and daughters are always welcome at home. Hispanics are expected to stay and help take care of our parents if that is what is required. This particular little tidbit is one of the principal reasons that it will be tough to sell the idea of the retirement home or managed care facility to Hispanics. It's not impossible to do, but I can guarantee you that the "We'll take care of them like you would," line just will not do it. Whether or not it is true, no one can take care of our parents the way we can and that's that.

PERCEPTION: Hispanics send money back home to support their families.

REALITY: Hispanics do send money back home. They add up to the second largest influx of dollars into Mexico, but today there is an additional consideration. As more products and services are effectively marketed to U.S. Hispanics an artificial need will be generated and more of their disposable income will go to buying these products and services, which will mean that most likely they will send less money home.

PERCEPTION: Hispanics love parties and they love reunions.

REALITY: We do love to have parties and reunions. You have to realize, however, that Hispanic parties and reunions are significantly different from mainstream parties. They last a lot longer and involve a lot more people—often the whole extended family. This is true of children's parties as much as it is true of adult parties. It seems to me that some of the wilder parties I have attended are for kids too young to know what is going on in the first place, let alone who was invited. I think it is this last point that made the parties as wild as they were. People got to invite whomever they wanted. After all Ramoncito wasn't going to object; why should anyone else?

In my experience with Hispanic parties I have found them to be a most effective way, if not the most effective way, that information passes from person to person and then gets disseminated beyond the party or reunion. It makes sense if you think about it. You have a large group of people that are surrounded by others they know and trust. Some of these people travel a long way for a good party. Once people leave they take what they heard with them and share it with friends and other family who didn't make the party because they were in a fight with Tio Chucho over a disagreement that took place 15 years ago. It is undisputable that community events and promotions reach more people, but based on what I have seen, when it comes to passing along information a Hispanic party or a reunion has yet to meet its match.

PERCEPTION: Hispanics love to go to the market as a family because they view this as a family outing.

REALITY: Who came up with that and how did they come up with it? I'd really like to know because in all my travels and conversations I have yet to hear this from a consumer. Most do in fact shop as a family, but for a variety of reasons. In my experience, a family outing is not included among these reasons. When we are talking about a less-acculturated Hispanic household, most of the time the reason they go to the market together has to do with perceived gender role expectations more than anything else. The husband or father in the house concedes the selection to his wife, who clearly knows more about the brands and products they use, and the mom concedes that it is the husband/father that doles out and regulates the money.

Notice by the way, that I said *perceived*. In many instances the woman is making as much, if not more, money than the man and she will still yield the issue based on what she believes her role to be. The kids, in most instances, come along because their parents do not have anyone to leave them with. If you want to take advantage of this dynamic to come up with something that turns the trip into an actual outing, do it. I think it is a good idea to leverage any instance in which you can speak to the family, but do not go into planning mode with the idea that they are already in that frame of mind and therefore delighted to partake in yet another activity that will extend their "outing."

PERCEPTION: Hispanic men tend to cheat on their wives more than other cultures.

REALITY: Again, I cannot speak with any authority in this regard because I do not have enough conversations under my belt about the subject to make definitive statements. Suffice it to say, that of all the couples I have spoken to, there had been an "issue" with more than three-quarters of them. I can also tell you that when it comes to my extended family, including grandparents, uncles, and cousins and the extended families of 95 percent of my closest friends, there also have been "issues." In every single instance within my family and in the majority of instances with friends' families and the people with whom I spoke, the female partner knew the situation was happening, but pretended at some point that it was not. In most of these instances there is indeed an unspoken sort of expectation that if you are male and you are Hispanic you are going to have a wandering eye and as long as you make it right by your family the attitude is "I don't care about what you do that I don't know." I would be lying if I said I have not seen a shift relative to these beliefs and ideas, but I would also be lying if I did not admit they exist. Again, something interesting to think about when you are hearing the echo of "Hispanics are all about family," that you have undoubtedly been fed time and time again.

Socioeconomics and Purchasing Power

PERCEPTION: Hispanics are generally from low to low-medium socioeconomic levels as well as from a limited educational background. This limits their ability to buy high-ticket items.

REALITY: Hispanics do come principally from low to low-middle socioeconomic backgrounds, but there is a huge difference in how that plays here in the U.S.

In our countries of origin, socioeconomic status has as much to do with the social aspect as it does with the economic aspect. People from the low to low-middle economic strata are perceived as belonging to the corresponding caste socially. It may not be something we talk about much, but we are aware it exists. In fact, it is possible that while you may have entered the high socioeconomic strata in your country of origin, you would still be considered to be of a lower social caste. In Mexico the vulgar way of referring to that caste is "Nacos." I guarantee you that upon reading this many of my Mexican compatriots might take umbrage at my assertion. I would only ask that they take two breaths and think about it and see if there is anything I am saying that is not true. It is uncomfortable to hear, but it is true.

When people come to this country they do come from that socioeconomic level, but over time they shed the perception that they will always be a part of it. One of the wonderful things about people coming to this country is that eventually there truly is an epiphany that takes place that allows most Hispanics who make it here to realize that anything really is possible. They also realize that there may be different classes of people, but there is no real caste system.

What does that mean in terms of marketing to Hispanics? A lot actually. Most marketers in the U.S. guide their planning by disposable household income, which is an entirely reasonable way of planning, particularly when it comes to high-ticket items. The problem is that while general market consumers may be driven by their ability to buy high-ticket items, many Hispanic consumers, particularly when it comes to high-ticket items, are driven by a disposition to buy and that is a big difference. By the way, some of the richest people in the world happen to be Hispanic. That is not a figurative comment either; it is literally the case. The Slim, the Azcarraga, and the Cisneros families are counted among the richest in the world. There is also a significant element of that money in the United States. San Diego, Los Angeles, Chicago, Denver, New York are all home to Hispanics whose average household income is measured in eight-digits.

PERCEPTION: Hispanics prefer things with which they are familiar. They are more brand loyal than the average at-large consumer and traditionally will sustain a brand across generations.

REALITY: Yes, Hispanics are brand-loyal, but no more than any other consumer. You would be brand-loyal too if the brand you were loyal to was one of two available to you. Once the brand repertoire opens up, you, like most of the Hispanics I have spoken to, would be interested in finding the best value for your dollar. All other things being equal, Hispanics will carry a brand from generation to generation if only a limited number of brands is available from generation to generation.

And speaking of value, just so we are clear when it comes to Hispanics, value is not determined by price alone. In fact brand in combination with price is what determines value. If it were just price, Hispanics would be some of the best consumers of house or generic brands and they are not.

Language and Media

PERCEPTION: Spanish-speaking Hispanics watch and listen to Spanish language radio and Spanish language television.

REALITY: As I think I made clear earlier in this book, what I have found is that although people who function in Spanish prefer to watch television in Spanish, they do so by a very narrow margin. Hispanic audiences are driven almost as much by content as by language fluency, which means they want high quality programming as much as they want Spanish-language programming. Whether or not we want to accept it, the current program line-ups on most Spanish-language networks are not high quality. It's not just me saying it; the audience says it. During my travels I had a chance to speak with a Telemundo TV talk show host, and I asked him what he watched. Guess what he answered? English networks. Yes, *novelas* are popular and we definitely do watch first division soccer from Mexico, but how many permutations of salacious variety shows can a person be expected to absorb? How many ways can you rename the same show where you have a young Hispanic throwing out Spanglish and playing the latest music? I counted three shows that are basically the same thing with a different name. Viewers resent that. They may watch some of that drivel, but they resent doing so, particularly young Hispanics who yearn to have something better represent their culture and interests.

PERCEPTION: Young Hispanics, those aged 15 to 25, love to speak Spanglish, a combination of English and Spanish, but they mostly speak Spanish when they are home.

REALITY: Spanglish is used by a significant number of Hispanics in the U.S., regardless of age. Let's start by defining what Spanglish actually is. Spanglish, in its most simple terms, is a combination of English and Spanish. Sometimes that combination means mixing the two languages in one word like *parkear* for parking or *carpeta* for carpet and sometimes it means mixing the two languages within one sentence. You would start the sentence in English or Spanish and finish it in the other language. It may be something like this: "I'm definitely going to the party *cuando termine de trabajar,*" which means, "I am definitely going to the party when I'm done with work."

Although Spanglish is used by Hispanics of all ages, it is those aged 15 to 25 that have made it an art form, flowing in and out of each language with a staggering fluidity. It is also in targeting these young Hispanics that most marketers use Spanglish. It is these same young Hispanics who nail these "hip" marketers who think they know how Spanglish flows and try to use it. It would be bad enough if they only tried to use Spanglish in broadcast media. At least in that instance with a good director and excellent casting, the flow of the Spanglish can be made to look and sound close to how it is really happens.

Please note that I did not include print in that media mix. The examples I wrote above actually look pretty lame to those they are most trying to target—Hispanic teens and young adults. It may sound good and seem like an easy fix, but trust me. I've been in a car full of Miami teens that read an ad for a large, American car company that is not GM or Chrysler that had Spanglish in it. For the next thirty minutes I could not get them away from talking about how stupid and lame the ad was and from asking: "Who do they think we are? Do they think that's how we really talk?"

When I pointed out, very humbly mind you, that they did in fact speak like that, what I got back was, "Yeah bro, but when we do it, it just flows. It comes without any planning. That's what makes it ours. Seeing it in writing just makes it cheap and fake and really pisses me off actually."

As far as what these young people speak at home, the truth is that they speak whatever they need to in order to be understood. In some instances that means fluent and correct Spanish, but most of the time it is English peppered with Spanish when they have to speak to their grandmothers or mothers. That may mean any of hundreds of permutations of bilingual elements, from single words spoken in Spanish or full communication in Spanglish.

So what language do you use to communicate with young U.S. Hispanics? I hate to say it, but it depends. It depends on the category, as well as the medium and the full confidence of the creative abilities of your advertising creatives. **However, you should never use Spanglish in print**. It looks and feels awful and it is one of the advertising elements that elicits the most violent responses from the very consumer you are looking to reach. In fact I got a weird vibe writing the example earlier in this section.

As I said, in hundreds of studies I have yet to come across an instance in which Hispanic young people say, "Hey that sounds just like us up on that billboard." Most of the time they let off a string of expletives I am embarrassed to print here. And by the way, while we are on the subject of print media, what is up with Hispanic magazines that are 95 percent in English and then there is a phrase or word in Spanish placed here or there? What's the reason for this? The magazine is mostly in English, so the readers most likely can read English. The readers also know from the titles, *Latina*, *Hispanic*, *Hispanic Business* along with the issues covered, that the magazines are aimed at the Hispanic reader. Why pander with a word or phrase here and there? I think it's great that these magazines have thrived and that many of their best articles are in Spanish and English, so why the cheesy "We have to show we are Hispanic" element?

PERCEPTION: There is a significant level of illiteracy or near illiteracy among foreign-born Hispanics.

REALITY: Hispanics from limited educational and socioeconomic background are "under-literate" rather than completely illiterate with the illiterate segment corresponding generally speaking to the very un-acculturated Hispanic. Why is this important? Does the word packaging do anything for you? If you believe your product will be sold to these consumers as its primary target then you might want to consider addressing their shortcoming through packaging that makes it easy for them to understand and easy for them to choose to use your brand.

Some foreign-born Hispanics do indeed come from a limited educational background, principally because they often have to begin working before they finish school. But there is also a significant population with growing influence of foreign-born Hispanics that come here to complete their undergraduate and graduate programs. In many instances they came here to study, but will stay here to raise their families. These are the Hispanics that we now see and hear about contributing some of the best thinking across fields. If you want hard evidence, feel free to visit *Latinogreeks.com* (a website dedicated to the Latino fraternity and sorority culture), and talk to the National Society of Hispanic MBAs. Ask them about the growth of their organizations and see what they tell you.

PERCEPTION: Internet usage among Hispanics lags significantly that of the at-large population.

REALITY: Well, yes and no. Internet usage among Hispanics lags the at-large population when it comes to the number of people that use the internet, but what about how long they stay on, how much they click-through, and how much information they pull once they are online? There are a number of measures that we can look at when we look at Hispanic online usage, but the undisputable one is the growth rate. Hispanics aren't suddenly becoming aware of the internet. We have always known it is there and used it, but you can't get on the internet without a computer and you can't get a computer if you don't know how much it costs (or worse if you think it costs more than it actually does), or where to get it, or what your options are.

Most high-tech companies, especially computer manufacturers, are still struggling to decide whether Hispanics represent a viable opportunity for them. After all, they don't really have the disposable income. Right? If you are with a high-tech company stuck in this predicament you would do well to remember the difference between ability to buy and disposition to buy because I can tell you disposition to buy will always outweigh ability. This attitude among high-tech companies seems to be changing, driven by a number of reasons not the least of which may be the cost of acquiring each new computer user in the at-large population versus the cost of acquiring each new user in the Hispanic population.

Financial Issues

PERCEPTION: Hispanics do not get credit, cannot qualify for it, and prefer to pay in cash in any case.

REALITY: This is partly true. Some Hispanics cannot qualify for credit since they do not have Social Security numbers. It is also true that they prefer to pay in cash. If you did not qualify for credit then you too would prefer to pay in cash since it is most likely the only way you can pay for the things you buy. Of the people I spoke with on the road, however, none that were asked about credit lacked an understanding, even if a basic one, of how credit works or how to use it.

The only time I remember hearing from consumers that they do not understand credit has been in instances in which we have recruited non-credit card users and somewhat risk-adverse people for research projects. Many credit card companies hear the cash thing and the "they don't get credit" thing and decide that offering information to Hispanics in the hope of making them cardholders is a lost cause. Therefore, they do not attempt to offer the consumer any information about their company and the vicious circle continues—no information, no applications.

What about the perception that Hispanics are credit averse? Again, I never heard that from actual consumers. I heard a lot about caution using it, caution obtaining it, and caution dealing with companies that offer it, but that does not make people credit adverse, it makes them cautious. You would be cautious too if you came from a country with an unstable economy and usury interest rates and you had companies here in the U.S. also preying on you with promises of cards for an upfront fee and more usury rates.

If you are a credit card company, how about providing the Hispanic consumer with the facts, for example:

- Most legitimate credit card companies do not ask for money up front.

- There are people out there willing to lend you some money at less than 30 percent, compounded monthly.

- There are protections in case the card is lost or stolen.

- Banks in the U.S. are regulated and also insured.

By doing the above you will be cutting through 90 percent of what makes some Hispanics "credit adverse" and you will be seeding the ground for the day you decide to do something more significant. Does this bring back Occam's Razor for you at all? It should.

PERCEPTION: Hispanics in the U.S. are under banked.

REALITY: One of the business categories most interested in understanding and tapping into the U.S. Hispanic market these days is the financial services category. Although this includes financial planning and investments, it is mostly the retail banks that are ramping up their efforts. As in the case of most companies, this has been spurred on by the growth of the market, but it has also been underscored by the belief that the U.S. Hispanic market is either under banked, meaning consumers use only a small part of what banks have to offer, or completely unbanked, meaning that they have no bank account.

Hispanics are indeed underbanked or unbanked. The principal reason is the requirements for opening a bank account. Many Hispanics do not have the identification or Social Security documents required. Some banks have been successful at resolving this issue by accepting an identification issued by the consulate of a customer's country of origin. Some states have begun making it difficult for banks to use substitute identification. What the rationale is still escapes me. Suffice it to say that in those states it has once again become an issue.

In their efforts to communicate with and to increase their Hispanic customer base, many banks have made serious investments in traditional advertising and marketing programs. This is excellent because a more informed consumer will always be a more open consumer. However, unfortunately for them, many banks have taken the same approach and developed similar programs, once again making it difficult to really stand out.

I can't tell you what the absolute answer is, but I can tell you what I have heard most often. Trust is an incredibly significant issue for these consumers, even the ones we would consider to be more acculturated and fully banked. Most often, their monthly statements and the charges they find on them generate the trust issues. This is where simplification would work wonders in my opinion—simplification and information about what the charges are.

I want to make clear that the issue is not that the charges are there. Most of the Hispanics I spoke with were willing to pay bank fees as long as they understood what they were for. It is worth noting that many of them mentioned the fact that they wouldn't mind paying for an all-inclusive monthly fee or package that is simple to understand. None of them mentioned having to be enticed or coaxed into opening an account by the promise of a free teddy bear or some other gift. We also know that many people who are not citizens or residents do have bank accounts. These may be people that come to the U.S. often, but do not live here and do not have any intention of doing so any time soon. How do they open bank accounts? They use a non-work-related Social Security number provided by the U.S., they use information and identification from their countries of origin, and a variety of other ways. Even though this is the case, I have yet to see a bank in the U.S. use this information to inform potential customers about how they can open an account.

From an investment standpoint, information is a critical component to communicating with Hispanics, as it would be with any consumer. The difference is that the information has got to come in the context of a relationship for the deal to be closed. Many of us that are more informed and more acculturated consider investing principally from a financial or monetary standpoint, but when it comes to picking a long-term planner the relationship definitely plays a role. For less-acculturated or less well-informed Hispanics this is multiplied tenfold. In this case, a financial planner becomes a facilitator for the process in addition to being an advocate and guide. I want you to notice that in every instance I have said relationship, not language or culture. Granted a Hispanic, Spanish-dominant financial planner has an easier time developing a relationship with a Spanish-dominant customer, but a patient, respectful, well-informed English-speaking planner also has an excellent opportunity to develop that relationship.

In two separate, unrelated stories, I heard from Hispanics in Los Angeles who made it a point to drive to a branch located further away from their house because it was a mainly an "American" branch. I was puzzled by this information so I asked what they meant. They explained that at their local, more Hispanic, Spanish-speaking branch the tellers were impatient and rude. They felt rushed through the transaction and in some instances they felt that they were a bother to the teller. A few went on to actually speculate that the tellers seemed to be ashamed of having to explain things in Spanish to them. They also explained that at the "American" branch the tellers were more patient and friendly and that they seemed to be truly interested in helping them out. As you can imagine I wanted to know how it was that they could be conducting this type of business when they themselves functioned in Spanish and that the tellers spoke principally English.

The answer I got was interesting and somewhat surprising at the time, but given what I heard many times during my travels, it makes sense. What they explained was that although they did function in Spanish, they had enough understanding of

English and enough ability to speak it to get through the transaction, particularly when they were working with someone interested in their business and who was patient about completing the transaction and answering their questions. They further explained that although the tellers were not bilingual, they too had enough grasp of Spanish to work through the transaction. In some instances the process actually engendered ongoing relationships between certain customers and specific tellers. So much so, in fact, that they told me that although they were not yet in the market for a mortgage or other services this would be the person they would first come to looking for information about them.

So if you happen to be in the financial services field and are interested in tapping into the U.S. Hispanic market you do have to pay heed to what you have no doubt been told at some point— developing a deeper relationship with U.S. Hispanics is a key to successfully selling these types of services to them. But, and this is a big *but*, if you were thinking that in order to do that you have to be bilingual, think again. Being respectful and patient may be more important than being bilingual. Being more fluent in Spanish will certainly be an advantage to you, but it is not a requirement.

Religion

PERCEPTION: Most Hispanics are baptized Catholic and whether they practice the religion or not, it forms a part of the culture.

REALITY: While the fact still remains that Hispanics are principally Catholic I think we need to understand the true nature of what that means. Given conversations with both Hispanic and non-Hispanic Catholics, I believe that being a Catholic is a different proposition for a Hispanic than it is for a non-Hispanic. To Hispanics being Catholic is a sort of birthright handed down from generation to generation. Your great grandparents were Catholic and so were your grandparents and parents and now you are too. You are a part of the fold, the tradition, and everything that comes with it. This may seem like an oversimplification and to those who practice the religion I apologize, but it is almost like saying, "I'm from Acapulco . . ." or "I'm from Caracas . . ." In most instances Hispanic Catholics participate in all of the special occasions that are tied to the church. First communion, baptism, and confirmation are all a part of what every Catholic child goes through. But aside from those special occasions and some others like Christmas and Holy Week, most Hispanics consider Catholicism to be more a part of their cultural make up than a religious practice. At least when we talked to them on the road they seemed to come back to culture way before coming back to religion. Aside from Catholicism, it is most definitely worth noting that other Christian religions are also finding an open and receptive audience among Hispanics, not only here in the U.S., but also in most countries of origin. Denominations such as Latter Day Saints, Presbyterian, and Methodist are finding open minds and hearts among some Hispanics who feel that the Catholic Church is too oppressive or unbending for our times, again their words not mine. Aside from Christian religions there is a healthy and vibrant Jewish community in Mexico, mostly clustered in Mexico City. As in the U.S., Mexican Jews have significant resources and significant connections into the places that make it happen. They are also some of the most vibrant and full-of-life people you will ever meet. Jehovah's Witnesses are also growing in significant numbers in both the U.S. and Mexico. In the interest of full disclosure I will say I adhere to an eclectic combination of Buddhist, Taoist, and California surf-culture beliefs.

Health

PERCEPTION: Hispanics diagnose their own health care problems, in part because they lack access to health care.

REALITY: We are most definitely self-diagnosers when it comes to health care. Actually, we say we are self-diagnosers because we are somewhat embarrassed about saying that our mom or some other relative or close friend was the one who provided the all-knowing diagnosis. The knee-jerk reaction would be to think that the reason for this is the lack of access to healthcare for many Hispanics in the U.S. and the fact is that you would be mostly, but not completely, correct.

There is a cultural aspect to it as well. It is the way we take care of things back home and when it comes to our mothers, it gives them the sense that they are taking care of us. This combination has in fact led to a lack of diagnosis of some of the most significant health problems for Hispanics, including cholesterol and diabetes. In addition, we have access to many medications in our countries of origin, which means that we are not only self-diagnosers, we are self-treaters as well (again, a bit embarrassing with mom handing you the pill).

The other thing I have heard about Hispanic health care is that Hispanics tend to use the emergency room as a doctor's office or a clinic. This also falls in the category of partially true. Many Hispanics do use emergency rooms and urgent care facilities as their primary doctor's office, but some of the reasons may surprise you. We have already covered the access issue, which does drive some of this, but not all of it.

There are three other significant reasons. First, the Spanish word for clinic is *clinica* and whereas in English it tends to lean more towards hospitals and other similar facilities, in Spanish it refers to the place where doctors are. Second, the doctor's office for which they have insurance or to which they have access may lack bilingual personnel. However, in most hospitals there is usually someone who speaks Spanish. Therefore, they go to the hospital for an accident and they get taken care of in Spanish and from then on decide that they would rather talk to someone in Spanish at the hospital than in English at the doctor's office. Third, because there is a lack of preventive medicine in most of our countries of origin we usually end up going because we are feeling symptoms, have already tried treating them, and have been unsuccessful at curing them, rather than because we want to keep in shape. If you think I am exaggerating about Hispanics and antibiotics, ask the closest Hispanic about them. See what they tell you. I can guarantee you that they have been given antibiotics as a result of a self-(mom)-diagnosis at least once in their lives, especially if they are foreign born. By the time I came into the U.S. at age 12, I had consumed more antibiotics than most people do in a lifetime. If you are a healthcare provider you have probably heard the "access, access, access" argument from here to eternity and yes, access to healthcare does play an important role, but it is not the sole factor.

Social and Political Issues

PERCEPTION: Hispanics come to the U.S. and take jobs from U.S. citizens. The jobs are usually blue collar or agricultural in nature.

REALITY: It is true that Hispanics, legal and illegal, come here and take jobs from U.S. citizens. Like immigrants that come from anywhere else, it is also true that they take jobs that most people who make this claim would never take. If you think I am exaggerating, go out to rural America and see who are the ranch hands in Montana, who are the strawberry pickers in California with their fingers raw from the acid of the berries. Go to those places and see who is doing those jobs–the immigrant. And if you do go there, notice that there will not be a line of displaced U.S. workers waiting to land those sweet jobs.

Hispanics do the jobs that most people do not want to do. They do it out of a sense of loyalty to the idea that one must do work—hard work, but honest work. There is no doubt that there are also lazy and unmotivated Hispanics that take advantage of the system. However, for the most part Hispanics come across the border for the same reasons that all immigrants, legal and illegal, take the risk to come to a foreign land. They want a better life.

PERCEPTION: Along with taking jobs, U.S. Hispanics drain the social services of the communities where they end up.

REALITY: Hispanics use the resources of the communities where they end up, but they also contribute greatly to them by bringing revenues and taxes, sometimes to towns that were largely dead. However, because of their legal situation, illegal Hispanics contribute a great deal to tax rolls that they never get back through tax returns. So once again, Hispanics consume resources, but they also subsidize many programs, which they do not qualify for if they are illegal. It amazes me that some people still believe that by denying illegal immigrants access to those things that address the most basic human needs they are solving the problem of illegal immigration. Remember the level of commitment we are talking about.

PERCEPTION: Hispanics in the U.S. seem to be constantly making claims of racism and oppression. Many individuals who have shared this perception with me feel the same way about African Americans and some other ethnic groups. They basically explained to me that every time they heard something about these ethnic groups it seemed to be in that context.

REALITY: While I cannot speak to the issue relative to the African American and other groups, I can tell you what I have come across relative to the Hispanic population. In all of my travels, in all of the studies and in all of the conversations I have had, the issue of racism and oppression has not come up once, unless I specifically bring it up. When I bring it up, I would say that only about one-half of one percent of the people to whom I have spoken have told me that they have felt discriminated against in one situation or another. Most of the time people tell me they are aware that it exists and that it does in fact happen to many

Hispanics, although they may not know of one person it has happened to. The most obvious question is: "So how do you know it exists and happens to a lot of people if it has never happened to you and you don't personally know anyone to whom it happened?" The response is always the same: "Because I saw it on the news." When I ask, "What news?" I again am told the same thing, "The Spanish-language news," which leads me to my next point. Based on what I have heard from people on the road and what I have had a chance to see personally, it seems that Spanish-language stations and networks spend a great deal of time reporting on and in some instances developing programming around the issue of racism and discrimination. The reason seems to be the sensational nature of the stories. Don't get me wrong, there are stories that deserve to be covered and that should serve to improve the conditions for many of these people, but given that it does not seem to be an issue for most Hispanics other than when it is thrust in front of their faces, it seems a bit overdone. I think some Hispanic advocacy organizations also contribute to the problem. Often it is these organizations that make the claim independently, not based on prevailing opinion. This dynamic really comes into play when we see ads on television using Hispanic icons or music and we then hear that some group or another has claimed it is offensive or inappropriate. In many instances I have had a chance to have a conversation with the Hispanics the ad is supposed to have offended and most of the time there is either complete indifference or regret that someone is making that claim whereas the target audience thinks the ad is funny or interesting.

PERCEPTION: Most Hispanics lean toward the Democratic Party.

REALITY: It is well known that any time there is an election, Hispanics are generally tallied up on the Democratic column, with the exception of the Cuban population in Miami, particularly when a Bush is on the ticket.

The principal reason for this is that overall, Democrats are the party associated with worker rights and social reforms aimed at helping those who are less affluent whereas Republicans are generally identified with tougher immigration laws and enforcement and advocacy for the rights of the more affluent. I don't mean to lecture you on civics, but I do want to make sure the issue is framed properly because there is a significant misunderstanding and a shift in this regard. If you don't believe me, ask Senator Kerry where his Hispanic swing vote went. Although Hispanics do identify closely with worker rights, we also have a strong pro-business mentality. We most certainly believe in government taking less rather than more, particularly since in some of our countries of origin the government takes everything but the kitchen sink while it is in power. This is as true, by the way, of the gardener with one employee as it is of the developer with 100 employees.

While there is most certainly an awareness of tougher immigration laws and enforcement, the folks I have talked to do not make the direct connection to the Republican Party that Democrats would like to see. The growing number of Hispanics on both sides of the aisle, coupled with an increased terrorist threat and the awareness that the first family has strong ties to the Hispanic community, has made it much more of a "government" issue than a specific party issue.

I also asked what people think when politicians from both parties either speak Spanish themselves or trot someone out to speak Spanish as part of their campaigns. Most people said it was "nice" and that it showed an interest in the Hispanic community. I should clarify here that these comments applied when the person speaking did so with decent Spanish. If the person spoke bad Spanish or did not carry a meaningful message beyond the fact of speaking Spanish, people considered it pandering and viewed it negatively. This was true, whether the politician in question was Hispanic or non-Hispanic. By contrast, when Hispanics were directly involved in the initiatives and platforms and showed true interest in and concern for the community either because they came from it or had some direct connection with it, most Hispanics reacted extremely positively, once again regardless of party.

As you can see, there is certainly not a 180-degree difference between perception and reality for the U.S. Hispanic. I have shown that, to a large extent, the perception of the Hispanic market is firmly grounded in how it really is. However slim the gaps may appear, the differences that do exist may be absolutely critical to your success with the U.S. Hispanic market. As the market grows in sophistication, it will be critical to success to understand those differences in-depth. Whether it is a 180-degree difference or a subtle distinction, bridging the gap between perception and reality will truly lead to success when marketing to Hispanics in the future. Finally, what this section should illustrate for you is the incredible opportunity that the U.S. Hispanic market holds for those who are willing to dig deeper and go with their instincts, even those who are not Hispanic and are not *supposed* to get it.

As with most researchers who have been at it for a while, I have interviewed or been in focus groups with thousands of consumers over the years. In the past two years, most of the conversations I have had with Hispanics have been outside of focus group facilities —in their houses, at their jobs, on the street, anywhere that would yield a true picture of who they are, what they do, and why. In spite of this, every time I begin to get even a remote inkling that I know what is going on, the consumer always shows me how far I am from complete understanding. These instances of complete wonderment and surprise from the consumer keep me passionate about what I do. The differences between what I hear from them and what I hear being pawned off as expert advice has been the inspiration for my writings thus far.

What Makes You Such an Expert?

In the interest of credibility I think I should share with you where all of this comes from. At the beginning of my career I didn't think about or study the U.S. Hispanic market. I was the marketing director for a company that marketed to consumers in the Southern California and Northern Mexico regions. I then began to think of the U.S. Hispanic marketplace as a distinct and unique set of consumers, so I thought I should understand them. This is when I was fortunate enough to come across Market Development (now known as TNS/Market Development.) Market Development was a research and consulting firm specializing in the Latin American and U.S. Hispanic markets. A brilliant Panamanian woman, Loretta Adams, founded it. She spent the better part of her career understanding and sharing her insights of the marketplace with major U.S. companies here and in Latin America.

I think the way the company has grown is a testament to Loretta and the research staff she put together. I was fortunate because my direct supervisor was a smart and open-minded woman by the name of Laurie Elliott. Roger Sennott, the late general manager of Market Development, had the most impact on my career. I believe that Roger was the first person in my career that showed me the incredible power that pure, unencumbered, and clear statistical brilliance can wield over any situation. Roger died in 2002 and every time I am faced with a tough dilemma, no matter the nature of the situation, his is still the first face I see when I am looking for an answer.

After that I got lucky once again and ended up at Cheskin Research and Consulting. Cheskin at the time was not at all focused on the Hispanic market as a separate and distinct opportunity. The company was founded in the 1950s and made a name for itself as a cutting-edge research and consulting firm that emphasized a real-life practical approach to understanding who the consumer was, regardless of ethnic background. So the bottom line at Cheskin was how do we understand and speak effectively to an audience, period.

We'll deal with the whole ethnicity thing as we need to, but let's understand these people as consumers first. It was the difference between how Cheskin approached understanding consumers and how Market Development did it that first gave me a glimpse of the huge gap between the general market and the Hispanic market when it came to real, usable consumer insights. Back then Cheskin did not have a specifically targeted Hispanic program, so most of the work we did that included Hispanics also included African-American and Anglo consumers. It was the opportunity to work on many such projects that shaped my beliefs relative to the similarities between Hispanic consumers and every other consumer group. These beliefs have contributed to many of the ideas and points of view that you have read in this book. I was also fortunate in that the CEO of Cheskin at the time, Christopher Ireland, had the vision to commit to grow the company's multicultural practice. I think most people that know Cheskin now know just how successful the company has been in establishing and expanding its reputation as a multicultural research consultancy that now includes Asian and Latin American capabilities.

The core of my training and experience was actually begun between Tacuba and Tecamachalco, two very different environments. As I mentioned before, one afforded me luxury and fine dining and the other offered me a fine butt-whipping every other weekend. In the U.S. I worked side by side in some very labor-intensive jobs with the very consumers I am trying to reach today. My time at W&O Supply, Arcwell Shipfitters, and Smart Tune Up were some of the hardest, bitterest, but most useful, learning anyone could hope to get. And truth be told, as hard as the work was, while working at these places I had some of the best laughs I've ever had. They truly were a major force in shaping my belief system and they form a part of what our agency draws from today—unabashed life.

Portraits

Edwin Sosa
Age 33, Brooklyn, New York

Hi, my name is Edwin Sosa and I am 33 years old. I came from the Dominican Republic almost 20 years ago with my mother and my grandparents. No, I am not related to Sammy Sosa (Although I have used that to pick up honeys at the club, you know what I'm sayin'?) We arrived in Brooklyn and have not left since. I speak English perfectly, but I still have a bit of accent a little bit of *sabor* to the way I speak and I speak Spanish perfectly although now it is more of the Spanglish variety.

Right now I am working for Delta at JFK doing baggage handling for them. The pay's good and since I live with my parents I save most of it. That's not really true. Aside from the traditional expenses for my social activities, you know what I'm sayin', taking the honeys out for a night on the town and for audio equipment, I do save up my money.

The most important thing I'm saving up for right now is my demo. I am going to make it big *papi*, don't doubt it! Right now its mostly Reggaeton, but I'm also mixing in some straight rap. It's going to be tight when I'm finished, you know what I'm sayin'? It's interesting the way the business works though. Sometimes I have to play my Hispanic side up and sometimes I have to play my black side up. Oh, I didn't tell you? Yeah man, I'm a Blacktino. If you saw me walking down the street I would look like any other brother from the neighborhood. It's something I've had to deal with my whole life, which one am I. Even my friends when we were younger would debate what we should

---

Portraits presented here are composites of people I interviewed on my trip. None is intended to represent a particular person.

really call ourselves. They are Blacktinos too, and man we had some bad fights over that right there. As I got older, as most of us got older, we started to realize that we could be both and that sometimes being both had its advantages.

I watch mostly English language television, but I do watch shows on Mun2 and some other channels that have music on, just to compare myself to what's out there. I get marketed to just like everyone else that has a Hispanic surname, in Spanish and to be honest with you if it ain't something I'm looking for I just tend to ignore it, you know what I'm sayin'? I'm Hispanic and all and I am very proud of the fact and wear my country's colors when I can, but I don't get into the whole Hispanic power shit, you know what I'm sayin'? That ain't what Edwin's about at all. I mean I'll use it to get ahead and to inspire my music, but there is no higher cause or Latino pride thing I want to be involved in. I think there are so many of us here in the U.S. now that it doesn't really make a difference. I also do a little bit of DJing on the side to make a little extra money for the finer things. A brother got to look good, you know what I'm sayin' especially when you are trying to get into the business and all. You can't walk around wearing fake shit cause you'll get spotted and forget about it man; from then on you'll be a punk wannabe.

My grandparents passed on a few years back so now it's just my moms and I. We make by OK with what she makes and what I make, but when I make it I am really going to set her up tight, you know what I'm sayin'? I mean after all the sacrifices she's made to get me to where I am and still be a decent enough guy. I love my neighborhood. We all grew up together here and we all have these great dreams of making it, even if some of us know that not everybody will. I'll tell you what I do a lot of and that's listen to the radio, boy do I listen to the radio. Everything and anything you can imagine I listen to. Of course I love my Salsa, my Merengue and my Bahcata, but I listen to everything.

RAP obviously. Did you know that RAP stands for Rhythmic American Poetry? I bet you didn't; most white folk don't. I listen to rock, to contemporary rock, classic rock anything man. And I'll dance to any of it too. I think it will make me stronger as a performer.

Well, we are getting to the end and I have been waiting to tell you my biggest secret. It's always very hard for me to open up about it, but it's a part of who I am and I am not ashamed of it. I was born a woman. My name was Erica Sosa and I had transgender surgery two years ago. It has worked extremely well for me because I always had a masculine look and always had very masculine tendencies. Even as kids the guys from around the neighborhood never treated me like a girl. Part of it may have been the fact that I could kick their ass every day to Sunday if they said anything. So when I went away for three years to have my treatment and my surgery completed and then came back to the neighborhood everybody took it like nothin' which was the best thing man. I can't tell you what I would have done if they had freaked. As you can probably already guess I had to wait until I either moved out for good or until my grandparents died before going through with this. They were just not going to be able to deal with it. My moms has been cool throughout. I think she always knew something was funky and she always used to tell me "Mija, as long as you are a good person." well now it's "mijo" but the philosophy is the same. Anyway, I'm running late for work and I have a DJ gig afterwards so it's going to be a long night. It's been cool talking to you. Take care and peace out.

9

What About Mañana?

O NLY RECENTLY have I come to some significant realizations about the future of the Hispanic market. Although studies, reports, and expert opinions are plentiful, few of them address the future of the U.S. Hispanic market, the trends, or how either might affect corporate America. Everything out there is about the past or the present. Here are the numbers and this is what they mean. That's it. While trend analysis and futures appear to be a significant component of the success in long-term planning for most of the top companies in the U.S., they appear not to be necessary to develop a significant strategy to address Hispanic consumers. If you want to come up with this type of information for Hispanics you are most likely relegated to tea leaf reading or shaman bone-throwing.

Strategic Planning (Not)

Here I must digress for a moment and address an issue that bothers me. I can't begin to tell you how many times we have been asked, after winning a new piece of business, to sit through a download that includes sharing the existing Hispanic strategy. We go through the planning session and we get to the Hispanic strategy section and I wait for the strategy part. I wait and I wait, and it never comes. What does come is a combination of brand information relative to the Hispanic market, maybe a positioning statement, the previous year's, maybe two years' creative all coupled with a string of executional elements planned for the year and finally a media plan. Whatever it is, it is not strategy.

Strategy by definition is a carefully devised plan with a primary long-term objective at hand. Strategic planning is the process in which all relevant intelligence is brought in and considered. It is the point at which decisions are made as to what is going to be a part of the strategy and what needs to be considered as a tactical element, which may or may not support the long-term strategy, but which still may be effective from the standpoint of short-term objectives. In most of my experience the Hispanic "strategy," as presented, is relegated to a group of these tactical elements combined with a creative approach. Seldom does the Hispanic strategy really reflect a defined long-term objective relative to the U.S. Hispanic market and what it will take to achieve it.

The way I see it, when we say Hispanic strategy we should be talking about the direction that the company must take and the considerations that must be given in order to position the company with Hispanic consumers in the long-term. The definition of long-term obviously varies from company to company, but it should be longer (and it is for the general market) than the next six months. The strategy should address several questions:

- Where is the company today as it relates to the general market?

- Where is it today as it relates to the Hispanic market?

- And, where do we want the company to be as it relates to the Hispanic market in the next two years?

These are the questions that will yield a strategy rather than a bunch of tactical ideas strung together. All this leads us back to the original topic of the section, trend analysis and futures in the Hispanic market.

As I mentioned at the beginning of the section, trends and futures are not a part of the Hispanic marketing realm at the moment. The reason for that, I believe, is that most experts and analysts in this area are afraid of getting it wrong. While Faith Popcorn and other experts like her are more than willing to go out on a limb and actually come up with some ideas about what the market holds in the future, those of us in the Hispanic marketing realm are busy making sure we get our analysis of the market right for today. We spend a lot of time on the census and other demographic figures and on analyzing existing programs, but we don't look at some of the trends that are shaping the market in which we work. We know the trends are there and we see them take shape, but we do not want to risk making a call and getting it wrong because in our business, cultural credibility is everything. I hope you noticed I write "we" here as I am a part of this group. Up until this book I have been firmly entrenched in the let's-get-today-right camp. But that's about to change.

My Crystal Ball

I'm going to share with you what I believe are some of the more significant trends I see relative to the Hispanic market. While I can't provide insight as to what they will mean for every single category I will try to contextualize from the standpoint of some important categories as well as from an overall business standpoint.

- **The role of Hispanic women will become vastly more varied and important in the culture.** The first point I want to share is the role that the Hispanic female will have in shaping the culture and the way it is perceived in the United States. We have talked about and looked at the role of women within the household forever and we have done so from the standpoint of household consumption. In that regard, we have pretty much stayed within established gender roles. As I mentioned earlier, women's influence on the culture has grown way past the front door of the house. In general, Hispanic females define themselves culturally at a much younger age and they are much more comfortable with their "Hispanicness" at a younger age than Hispanic males. I see this dynamic clearly when I speak with Hispanic teens and tweens. Whereas Hispanic males may still be struggling to define themselves culturally, Hispanic females have already done so and are on the way to defining themselves professionally and socially.

I can't tell you how many times I have spoken with 13-to-15 year-old Hispanic males who can do no better than, "I dunno," when I ask them their thoughts and ideas about the future and what they plan to do. Hispanic females, on the other hand, some as young as 10 to 11 can easily articulate what their plans are, if and where they plan to go to school, and how they plan to get things done. I believe this has translated into an important and real dynamic that is yielding great leadership across a host of backgrounds. It has most obviously meant a significant role for Hispanic women in politics at the local and national levels, a significant role for Hispanic women in business where Hispanic women occupy positions on corporate boards and in senior management in Fortune 500 companies, and from an entrepreneurial standpoint with Hispanic women occupying the number one spot when it comes to new businesses opening in the United States.

I mention this trend first because I think that being able to communicate successfully with Hispanic women will yield immediate tactical success. In addition, given their growing influence on the overall culture and on Hispanic youth through their roles as mothers, sisters, and friends, communicating with Hispanic women in a meaningful way will yield a strong strategic base that will provide companies with advocates and mavens to carry their brand or product messages across generations. As we think about how we realize growth in the next 3 to 5 years, marketers will be well served to look beyond the traditional homemaker definition and consider the Hispanic woman as a thought-leader and cultural influencer. Or we can ignore the trends, stick with the way we consider Hispanic women, and watch as the competition leaves us behind.

- I believe that the balance between bilingual/English dominant and Spanish dominant will stay at about 65 percent bilingual/English dominant and 35 percent Spanish dominant. I also believe that if we analyze the changes in this balance, we will notice that they shift in both directions with the numbers on either side getting larger and smaller over time, rather than having them change in a linear fashion. Recent research shows that approximately 60 percent of the U.S. Hispanic population is either bilingual or English-dominant. Like all numbers related to the Hispanic market, this share varies from source to source, but this 60/40 split is most likely the best reflection of who speaks what as of today. This compares with 52 percent bilingual and 48 percent Spanish-dominant just three years ago. You may believe the shift in shares is due to more people becoming fluent in English and therefore defining themselves as being bilingual. Or you may believe that the shift will continue with more people becoming bilingual over time so that eventually the split between bilingual and Spanish-dominant might be more like 70 percent to 30 percent. However, I believe this would be a mistake. The more time people spend here the more likely it is that they will become bilingual, but as we have seen it doesn't necessarily have to be the case. Although the balance within the existing population might change with time, we know there are new immigrants coming across the border every day, and regardless of what the government might wish, they are going to keep right on coming.

- As Hispanics have more access to credit they will be more likely to purchase high-ticket items more quickly and without as much planning. Unfortunately, this will also mean that more Hispanics will have financial difficulties and perhaps even consider bankruptcy. Although the numbers will grow in this regard, it will be principally due to the increase in numbers accessing credit, not to a specific cultural proclivity. In fact Hispanics are likely to be excellent credit customers since most understand that having good credit will help them establish themselves further in the United States.

- **The numbers of Hispanic white-collar workers will grow significantly as more young people graduate from college and begin careers in corporate America.** Expectations relative to recruitment and hiring will shift along with this increase. As more Hispanic executives are in place and performing well, more Hispanics will have greater opportunities based on growing interest in capturing the U.S. Hispanic market.

- **The Hispanic presence in politics will become significantly more prominent.** With a Hispanic Attorney General, a Hispanic Secretary of Commerce and a Hispanic mayor of Los Angeles, I don't really think I'm going out on a limb making this call. However, based on what I heard on the road, I do think that the alignment of the Hispanic population with the Democratic Party will be severely strained. As the Republican Party continues to place more conservative and Christian values at the forefront of its platform, Hispanics are likely to be more open to its message since it lines up with many of their own values.

- Even though I would like to be wrong in this regard, **I believe that the high-tech industry, most notably computer manufacturers, will still lag when it comes to communicating with the U.S. Hispanic market.** This dynamic is unlikely to change until one of the more prominent high-tech players decides to embark on a long-term sustained initiative targeting U.S. Hispanics. This continues to baffle me. When you think about the cost of acquiring each new computer user in the general population and the cost of acquiring a new computer user in the Hispanic population it should be a no-brainer.

- I believe that the biggest and most significant evolution of the Hispanic market in the next five years will be due to the change and evolution of the media that is offered to them. If there is one thing that became clear throughout my travels and across previous conversations it is that even though they may not articulate it, the vast majority of Hispanics yearn for more choice. I believe those choices are coming and as they do the overall expectations of the Hispanic audience will also change. Gone will be the days when Hispanic consumers have three choices, *novelas,* soccer, or the news. As channels like Discovery, History, A&E and VH1 become more ubiquitous, the Hispanic audience will demand the same quality from the Hispanic networks. As with everything else, these networks are free to ignore the trend, but they will most likely suffer significant consequences as a result. Added to this pressure, Hispanic networks are also likely to see English-language networks as well as cable channels used more as vehicles for Spanish-language advertising.

- Hispanic women will continue to join the workforce in ever-growing numbers and they too will continue to fill more significant roles as part of the white-collar, executive work force. Hispanic women will continue to grow in numbers as small-business owners and will in fact expand their reach as they become better versed in categories like financial planning, tax advice, and travel, given that these categories are among those that more Hispanics will need.

- Hispanic youth between ages 16 and 25 will undergo a significant evolution driven by the change in the media landscape outlined above. Actually, it won't be so much that their attitudes will change, but it will be easier for them to voice their points of view based on additional venues that may be more aligned with their interests and attitudes. As more options become available, bilingual and even English-dominant young

Hispanics will be more open to consuming Spanish-language programming which will mean that over time they may define themselves as being bilingual, very much along the lines of what we touched on earlier when we covered the balance in language fluency. Additionally, Hispanic youth will also move within a more eclectic mixture of cultures. These will include African-American and Asian culture, as well as elements of what defines popular culture like the extreme sports culture or the hip-hop culture. Watch California to see this trend emerge.

- As far as the population split is concerned, while the Central and South American population will continue to grow and will become a more significant component of the Hispanic culture in the U.S., geographic reality means that the majority of the U.S. Hispanic population will continue to be Mexican. I think that the most significant shift will indeed be the growth of the Central and South American population, which combined may outstrip the Puerto Rican population in markets like Chicago. We will need to keep a close watch on the markets that have traditionally defined as Hispanic markets in order to ensure that what we believe the mix of Hispanic cultures to be actually reflects the population in each market.

These are only some of the trends that are clearly taking shape when it comes to the U.S. Hispanic market. There are a lot more trends that will be significant for corporate America and that should not be difficult to define if someone is willing to look.

Portraits

Margarita Gonzalez Peres
Age 52, Phoenix/Tucson, Arizona

My name is Margarita Gonzales Peres and I am 52 years old. I originally came from Peru 25 years ago. I am an American citizen now. I am also an adjunct professor of Hispanic Studies at the University of Arizona. I am married and I have three grown children and two beautiful grandchildren.

My culture is incredibly important to me; it forms a part of who I am and how I lead my life. Being Hispanic in this country has not been easy and that's what I think young people forget sometimes. I think sometimes they forget the sacrifices of all those people in decades past that used to plant and pick the fields in California. They forget the fact that it was on the backs of those people that one of the most powerful states in the union was built. Now days young people have it easy; they are free to speak Spanish wherever and whenever they want and they do not give it a second thought when they dress in those disgraceful outfits falling down to their waist, showing their underwear and the girls wearing those tight pants. You see most of these kids do not understand that even today we are still in a struggle, the same struggle we have been in for thousands of years. Our language and our culture are fundamentally under attack. Under attack by those that see us as just an opportunity to make money and who would bastardize what we have built over time for the sake of peddling their wares.

Of course I watch Spanish television, the news mostly because I don't have time with my teaching schedule. I do also

---

Portraits presented here are composites of people I interviewed on my trip. None is intended to represent a particular person.

watch English language television, just a couple of shows, *The Sopranos* and *Deadwood*, even though *Deadwood* is really historically inaccurate since it doesn't show the heavy indigenous influence from the North of Mexico. I find it absolutely amazing that people here are completely willing to overlook and forget the fact that the U.S. stole what is now California, Arizona, and New Mexico from the Mexican government. Actually they didn't steal it; they extorted for it. Let's see, Santa Ana was forced to give up the land in order to get the U.S. government to withdraw the U.S. troops from the capital city. Of course they took over the city after doing battle with mere kids at the Military Academy in Mexico. I know it was all a long time ago. I am a professor of Hispanic studies, *por el amor de Dios*! I get so upset that these kids don't know who Cesar Chavez, Joaquin Murrieta and even Pancho Villa were.

I try to buy mostly Mexican brands because that's what they have the most of in the neighborhood I live in and I will support everything that is *lo nuestro* you know; we have to help each other.

Everyday across the country abuse takes place. Sometimes they get caught on the news, but then what about all of those that don't? That is what organizations like the National Council on La Raza are there to try to eradicate, but we first have to play our own small part in the community by standing up for ourselves when we are being discriminated upon.

10

A Final Word

ERE WE ARE once again at the end of our journey. If you read *The Whole Enchilada* then you know this journey was a bit more turbulent, but I hope you will agree it is one we had to take. I wanted to leave you with some final thoughts about some of the ideas in the book, on the journey I went through, and on what it all means.

Whether you agree with anything I have shared with you, everything I have written in this book is my personal take on what I have heard and seen over the years. I have truly been fortunate to speak with so many people in so many places and I have tried throughout this book to maintain the integrity of what I have heard, even in instances in which it was in complete conflict with my preset notions or hypotheses.

I hope that you have also gotten the sense that I have a lot invested in what I do and that it is more to me than just business. I am passionate about what I do and truly hope to effect a change in the way corporate America thinks about marketing to Hispanic consumers. In the end, however, I will be satisfied if even one company or one executive uses the information to understand us better. I also hope that whether or not you agree with me, at the least I have made you question some of the preconceived ideas and notions you had about the Hispanic culture.

Ultimately and perhaps most important to me, I hope that the book has done justice to the eclectic and fascinating culture of U.S. Hispanics in a new millennium. If nothing else, being on the road taught me that just when we think we have things figured out, the ever-changing and unpredictable factor called life comes along and changes things. From talking to Hispanic billionaires to getting the best Mexican pastry I have ever eaten, including pastries in Mexico, from a couple in Passaic, New Jersey, the road was a true learning experience for me. The best Mexican pastry in Passaic, New Jersey! Need I say more?

I want to end this book by once again paying tribute to those individuals that through the skin of their teeth, through trials and tribulations, and costs both human and financial make the journey to the United States. Like many other Hispanics, I wish that their journey was safer and legal, but again life has taught us differently. I want to pay a small tribute to those individuals that died in May of 2003.

They are:

Mexico	Marco Antonio Villaseñor *(five years old)*
	Jose Antonio Villaseñor
	Serafin Rivera
	Roberto Rivera
	Héctor Ramirez
	Jose Luis Ramirez
	Elisendo Cabañas
	Edgar Gabriel Hernandez
	Juan Carlos Castillo
	Ricardo González
	Oscar González
	Catarino Gónzalez
	Juan José Morales
	Mateo Salgado
	Chelve Benitez
	Rogelio Domínguez
Honduras	José Felicito Figueroa
El Salvador	José Mauricio Torres
Dominican Republic	Stanley Augusto Vargas

Through your sacrifice you have once again proven the resiliency and indomitable spirit that no doubt drives most of the Hispanics that make it into our communities every day. I am proud to be Mexican, to be Puerto Rican, and to be a U.S. Hispanic. I am also proud of having the opportunity to work side by side with professionals that are just as committed and just as passionate about what we do.

To those of you in the Hispanic marketing, advertising and media industries that I do not know, but who may relate to some of the things I have shared with you I say this: Keep your chin up, even when you still get asked, for the thirtieth time, "What's so Hispanic about that?" Things are already changing. Continue to produce great work and good things will follow. They always do if we let them.

To you I also want to extend an invitation to join me in the effort of changing the mentality we have to deal with every single day. Whether it is by joining us here at Cultura (we are always looking for people as crazy as we are), or through the work you do at your own agency or within your organization. It has been a pleasure sharing these ideas with you, even if they did not all hit home for you. You are, believe it or not, what motivated me to write this book and what continues to inspire me to get better information and to do better work. I hope you enjoyed reading the book half as much as I enjoyed writing it.

Until next time, live well, have patience, and remember that when life throws you a curve, the best thing to do is smile to yourself and think, *asi viene el sandwich, men, asi viene el sandwich.* (That's the way the sandwich comes man, that's the way the sandwich comes). Until next time, *buen probecho* and enjoy!

About the Author

JUAN FAURA, President and CEO, founded CULTURA LP in 1999. While many in the industry felt that the market could not support another Hispanic advertising agency, Juan knew there was a niche for a forward thinking group who could make a distinct change in the establishment. Within two years, Cultura was one of the fastest growing Hispanic agencies in the country. Now in 2005 Cultura is an established Hispanic agency on the verge of another expansion and its leader shows no signs of slowing down.

Juan has over 15 years experience in advertising, marketing and research, and is a published expert on the Hispanic market, having published the book *The Whole Enchilada: Hispanic Marketing 101* as well as numerous articles, columns and opinion pieces on Hispanic marketing. He is also a frequent speaker and lecturer on Hispanic marketing at various conferences and universities. His books and articles are based on insights gained over his career through conversations with over 70, 000 Hispanics across the U.S. and a range of ages, genders, cultural, language and socioeconomic backgrounds. His credentials include positions as the Director of Global Strategy for Cheskin Research and Director of Research for Market Development, Inc. Juan has also served as a consultant on Hispanic marketing for Fortune 100 companies such as Hershey, Pizza Hut, Ortho McNeil, Ford, Neutorgena, Zubi Advertising, J&J, Hormel, Pepsi, Visa, Wells Fargo, Frito-Lay, Labbatt's (Tecate) and Mercedes Benz among others. He has also worked at a bakery, been a pipe fitter, a mechanic and a paint and body man.

Juan holds a Doctorate of Juris Prudence from Thomas Jefferson School of Law and a certificate in welding and sheet-metal handling from the Urban League in San Diego. He lives in Southlake, Texas with his wife Sara his children Juan, Amanda, and Sebastian and his three Boxer dogs Bongo, Memphis, and Lola.